Starting Small, Investing Smart

WHAT TO DO
WITH $5 to $5,000

Starting Small, Investing Smart

WHAT TO DO
WITH $5 to $5,000

Donald R. Nichols

Second Edition

BUSINESS ONE IRWIN
Homewood, IL 60430

Library of Congress Cataloging-in-Publication Data

Nichols, Donald R.
     Starting small, investing smart: what to do with $5 to $5,000 /Donald R. Nichols.—2nd ed.—Homewood, Ill.:Dow Jones-Irwin, c1988.
     x, 145 p. ; 24 cm.
     Includes bibliographical references and index.
     ISBN 1-55623-041-9   ISBN 1-55623-381-7 (pbk.)

     1. Investments—Handbooks, manuals, etc. I. Title.
HG4527.N53   1988   332.6'78—dc19   87-71258
Library of Congress   AACR 2 MARC

Printed in the United States of America

1 2 3 4 5 6 7 8 9 0 K 7 6 5 4 3 2 1 0

This book is for three friends who have given of their time and talent that I might make better use of my own:

George A. Chambers, Ph.D.
Charles A. deLeon, M.D.
Carl H. Klaus, Ph.D.

And most of all for my wife Barbara.

CONTENTS

Introduction

This is the second edition of *Starting Small, Investing Smart,* and although much has changed since the first edition—mostly tax laws—the premise of this book hasn't: Someone with less than $5,000 to invest has access to as many types of promising investments as someone with $5 million, and investment knowledge is the first step to investment profits.

Small investors have more investment alternatives available today than at any time in the history of 20th-century American financial markets. Consider the conventional stock mutual fund. As recently as 1950, mutual funds required a minimum investment of $5,000 to $25,000 to purchase shares in a diversified portfolio of common stocks—and even if you could come up with that price ante, your choices were largely restricted to blue-chip common stocks. Today, $50 to $2,500 is all that's required to invest in a stock fund, and there are not only thousands of funds, but also there are scores of different types of funds investing in different kinds of stocks.

The same with bonds. Since the 1970s, bond funds have exploded in both number and variety, and today $1,000 to $2,500 can situate you in corporate, government, municipal, convertible, zero coupon, and international issues.

As for the growing savvy of small investors, look no further than the incredible acceptance of money market funds. In 1970, the U.S. Treasury raised the minimum price of Treasury bills from $1,000 to $10,000, effectively throwing small investors out of that instrument.

Then along came a bright commoner who wouldn't accept that investors' returns should be governed by their bank balance instead of intelligence. He or she reasoned that if a T-bill costs $10,000 you could locate 10 small investors with $1,000 and all could own part of a high-yielding investment. From that idea sprang money market funds, and once available, many more than 10 small investors recognized their profitable advantages.

Unfortunately, financial authors too often deny the intelligence of small investors. They prefer to write about *surefire* formulas for quick riches instead of presenting alternatives to be weighed with judgment. One exception to that preference is *The Intelligent Investor* by Benjamin Graham.[1] Mr. Graham was a classics student who started in the investment business by running errands at a brokerage house, and he finished his career as senior dean of security analysis. His book is subtitled, "A Book of Practical Counsel," and among its practical counsel is that the first step in making money is not to lose it.

Mr. Graham's counsel is called *preservation of capital*, but divested of syllables it means a dollar under a mattress will be there when you change sheets. If you leave it under the mattress, it may lose purchasing power, but you'll still have the dollar, and that's the first step in making the dollar grow.

Theorists question whether the Washington Slept Here Theory of Capital Preservation really constitutes investment, but we needn't indulge questions about one theoretical hand clapping. We want to make money on what little cash we can set aside, and that's investing in anybody's book. How much cash is a little? As our title says: $5 to $5,000.

Returns we hope to receive from investing are *unearned income*, also called passive income in the post-1986 tax laws. Unearned income differs from *earned income*—payment for labor—in that it's investment income. When you work for your money, you have earned income; when your money works for you, you have unearned income. We'll investigate three types of unearned income: interest, dividends, and capital gains.

---

[1]New York: Harper & Row, 1973.

Interest is payment for lending money. Take $5 and open a savings account. The banker will lend your $5 and pay you interest for use of your $5. Lend money to a corporation, a city, or the federal government via buying a bond, and each will pay you interest, as we'll see in the chapter on bonds.

Dividends are payments by a corporation to people who own its common and preferred stock. Many payments are erroneously called *dividends*, and the term has come to mean any benefit from investment. We, however, use *dividend* in its legitimate meaning of payments by corporations to stockholders.

There's another sense in which we use the term *dividend* because the Internal Revenue Service insists, and that refers to income from mutual funds. As we'll see, mutual funds invest in several kinds of investments, some paying interest rather than dividends. Nonetheless, the IRS often interprets returns from mutual funds as dividends even if returns are paid to the mutual fund as interest. So sometimes we have to call income from mutual funds dividends.

Capital gains are income from selling something at a price higher than you paid. If you buy stock for $5 and sell it for $25, you have $20 in capital gains. Buy a gold coin for $35 and sell it for $435, and you have $400 in capital gains. The same is true for purchase and sale of a house, real estate, stamps, poems, and any other investment.

As we track unearned income, our Sherpa guide is The First Dictum: *Every investment has advantages and disadvantages.* The First Dictum is universally true, and that's why so many investment alternatives abound. Along with The First Dictum, other matters need to be remembered.

Investment is done with money you don't need right away. After bills are paid, after you've bought car and home insurance, after you anticipate expenses and earmark cash for them, then you invest.

Another consideration is that we're pursuing regular, more-or-less predictable returns from investment. Our first goal is not to lose money; our second is to accumulate relatively predictable unearned income. Nonetheless, many unstable and unpredictable investments are included because they're available to small investors.

Finally, we want safety and liquidity, albeit in degrees. Safety is relative certainty we won't lose what we've invested—seeking minimal market risk—and liquidity is ability to convert an investment to cash. In pursuing unearned income we trade among these considerations, perhaps accepting less safety for more income or less income for more liquidity.

What kind of people are "we"? We work for our money, and we have extra because we denied ourselves consumption. If we have stock options or employment sweeteners, it's because our employer gives them to everyone. Some of us are well educated but never learned about investments. Some of us will earn more than others and will graduate to sophisticated investments. But right now, we're beginning investors.

What returns are possible for people like us? Conservatively, we can double our money two or three times in a lifetime if we're around 50 years old, and we can do better than that if younger.

Given limitations of our financial situations, this book omits a number of investments. It doesn't discuss selecting specific stocks, although it discusses direct and indirect ownership of stocks. It does not discuss investments requiring more than $5,000 or esoteric investments like stamps and rugs, nor does the book discuss complex tax-advantaged investments.

This second edition of *Starting Small, Investing Smart* is still a nuts-and-bolts book for meat-and-potatoes people. It tries to be educational by informing investors of choices open to them and of consequences of their choices. Miscellaneous considerations are thrown in with the hope they're helpful, and the book's fondest hope is still that every reader will outgrow its fundamental counsel.

Risks

Every investor must accept risk. When financial institutions claim that an investment with them is risk free, pay no attention because there is no such thing as a risk-free investment. The best that one investment can do over another is offer a different type of risk in exchange for a different possibility of reward.

Most investors define risk as "losing what I invested." In the more careful vocabulary of investments, that's a specific risk—market risk. *Market risk* is the possibility your investment will be worth fewer absolute dollars than you initially invested. Minimal market risk is called safety.

There are several subdivisions within the category of market risk. They may include risk associated with the overall economy, with a particular industry, or with a specific firm, and you may see them called *business risk*. But they all accumulate to influences that threaten to reduce the number of dollars you initially invested.

When banks say a savings account is risk free, they really mean "free from market risk." Give a bank or a savings and loan a dollar, and it must, by law, preserve your dollar. However, that won't guarantee your dollar will always be worth a dollar as measured by goods and services you can consume with it. Failure of investments to preserve worth is called *loss of purchasing power* and the risk in question is *purchasing power risk* or *inflation risk*.

You've heard how purchasing power risk is *said* to work.

Invest a dollar in a savings account paying 5 percent simple interest, and at year's end you have $1.05. However, if the general rate of inflation averages 10 percent, you'd have had to have earned 10 percent interest merely to stay even. Therefore, or so the argument usually runs, your investment has lost money because you can't buy as much with it as you could have bought a year earlier. This argument is not accurate, but more about it in a moment.

Tax-rate risk hooks up with inflation risk. In the last example we invested a dollar, giving us $1.05 at year's end. We supposedly saw, however, that inflation had averaged 10 percent for the year, so that we were generally thought to have lost money. Then in walks the tax man. If we happen to be in the 20 percent federal tax bracket, we owe Uncle Sam a penny of the nickel earned as interest—and that's before the governor, the mayor, and the sewer district commissioner walk through the door with their palms up. To be rigorous, taxes aren't risks as defined by the investors' dictionary. Risk is calculated acceptance of uncertainty, and there's nothing uncertain about taxes. You can postpone paying them sometimes, but you or your estate must eventually render unto Caesar.

Another form of risk is interest rate risk. *Interest rate risk* is often mentioned as a subcategory of other types of risk, but interest-bearing investments have become so popular that interest risk deserves to stand forth as its own ogre. Interest rate risk has three parts.

The first is failure to receive anticipated interest. Although that might happen because the interest payer goes broke (default risk), it may also happen because he or she fails to make as much money as expected with cash borrowed (business risk) and because the general level of interest rates was lower than expected.

The second aspect of interest rate risk is *reinvestment risk.* If you lock cash into one investment and interest rates rise, you might be stuck with its lower rate of interest while everyone else earns higher current rates. On the other hand, if you buy a bond paying 12 percent interest, and when it matures the best rate is 5 percent, you've lost 7 percent interest because you can't reinvest at past levels.

The third aspect of interest rate risk pertains to *fixed-*

payment investments such as bonds. The problem is that interest rates change and interest payments don't. Because investors always want returns consistent with present levels, prices of fixed-payment investments fall as interest rates rise, linking interest rate risk to market risk. Of course, they also rise as interest rates fall. More about this in the chapters on bonds.

Throughout discussions of various investment vehicles we'll mention each of these risks as they apply to particular investments. However, inflation has been such a prominent worry, and so many institutions proclaim themselves "the best hedge against inflation," that the subject of inflation risk deserves an expansion.

When economists talk about inflation they generally discuss one of two events. First, by *inflation* they may mean "any increase in the supply of money." You've heard the definition of inflation as "too much money chasing too few goods," with the consequence that prices of goods rise when confronted with all that money chasing them. This leads to the economists' second definition of inflation as "any sustained increase in the general price level."

When economists speak of the *general price level*, they are referring to an index which is said to represent a standard market basket of goods and services. When you read in the newspaper that the consumer price index (CPI) rose or fell, you are being told that prices of goods and services comprising the index rose or fell, and from those movements comes a blanket statement about inflation.

Both definitions are generalities that do not necessarily pertain to individual investors and consumers. To some extent, we each have our own inflation rate, which may be greater or less than the norm. Peculiarities of region, personal tastes, position in the life cycle, and personal lifestyle influence our personal rate of inflation, and they may make it considerably less than the measured norm. Of course, these considerations may elevate our personal rate of inflation above the average.

Let's say that three items contained in the inflation index are the price of steak, the price of a house, and the price of a new car. In this case, the index corresponds to inflation for a carnivore who's buying a new car and house, not the inflation rate of the vegetarian renter who commutes by train.

In addition, discussions of inflation fail to consider higher income and reduced consumption. Most of us will make more money as we age, and often wages are tied to an inflation index. And we do spend less at different times in our lives. Therefore, inflation may not be as ravaging in personal and investment consequences as we're led to believe.

Also, products improve. The price of a car in 1987 is higher than in 1950, but a 1987 car is a better product—or at least a different product. So when you're told your investments are suffering because inflation has eroded your purchasing power, consider what you're buying.

The message is not that inflation is no concern. Rather, the message is that we must invest with regard for personal circumstances, not with regard to generalities thrown about in name of "purchasing power" and "hedges against inflation."

Alexander Pope wrote "Know then thyself," and that's a good rule to follow in considering both your vulnerability to inflation and your willingness to accept investment risks. Perhaps you needn't be deeply concerned about inflation in your investment choices, but if you're going to invest at all you will have to accept some type of risk. Fortunately, the variety of investments is large enough to permit small investors to choose not only the returns they want, but also the risks they wish to accept.

Investing in Yourself

Glossaries of investment books often don't include entries such as "nose job, see rhinoplasty," but they should. Each of us is our principal asset in this world, and anything we do to improve ourselves will add to our personal capital as well as financial capital.

Eighteenth-century philosophers believed human beings were perfectible, that we could be improved as a sculptor could polish marble or an author a sentence. The notion that people are improvable, if not perfectible, lives on. Go to the bookstore and observe the self-improvement titles. Open a matchbook and see what correspondence course is offered therein.

Investments in schooling or personal improvement might provide greater income than another investment of similar cost. To say so requires stretching the concept of investment, but not by much. If you take a night school course that increases your salary $2,000 a year, you'd have to invest $40,000 at 5 percent to achieve the same return. Similarly, for a receptionist with a thick accent, a bald salesman of sporty autos, or a pathologically cranky middle manager, diction lessons, a toupee, or psychoanalysis may improve income (as well as self-presentation and personality) more than conventional investments.

Money spent to improve employability and performance might be the most profitable investment you could make. For people tenuously employed in withering occupations this may be the only sound investment to make. Here's a thought from

George A. Christy and John C. Clendenin in *Introduction to Investments:*[1] "Extending one's education or personal skills may call for a considerable outlay of money, strenuous effort, and substantial sacrifices of family and social life, but almost invariably it more than repays these costs."

---

[1]New York: McGraw-Hill, 1974.

CHAPTER FOUR

Deposits in Banks, Savings and Loans, Credit Unions

Depository institution and *depositary* are broad names including all financial institutions that accept deposits and put those deposits to work through loans. Although there are many types of depository institutions, some—such as mutual savings banks and Morris Plan banks—are lesser known or are localized in selected regions of the country. Therefore, we'll concentrate on three types of depository institutions most familiar and available to depositors: commercial banks, savings and loans, and credit unions.

The first thing you need to understand about depositaries is that every deposit you place in a depository institution is a loan. The institution takes your money and lends it to other people, and sometimes it doesn't pay you interest for lending your money. Conventional checking accounts are interest-free loans to your bank or S&L.

NOW ACCOUNTS

What we want is interest from loans we make to banks, and the first kind of interest-paying loan you can make to a bank is through a special checking account called a *NOW account.*

NOW stands for "negotiable order of withdrawal," and essentially NOW accounts are interest-bearing checking accounts. They function as do conventional demand deposit accounts—with printed checks and running balances and regular statements—except that they pay interest. Interest differs among institutions, with 5 percent being the norm. However, beyond that standard, other requirements vary considerably.

First, there's often a minimum balance requirement of up to $2,500, with $500 to $1,000 being a common range. Depositors are expected to maintain a certain specified amount in their accounts, even though you could be earning higher interest elsewhere. Further, some institutions require a constant absolute minimum in NOW accounts, whereas others require an average monthly or quarterly balance.

Second, in addition to differing in interest paid and in required minimums, NOWs differ in the way they pay interest. One institution may pay monthly interest on the average balance, a second may pay daily interest on the daily account balance, a third may pay interest from day-of-deposit-to-day-of-withdrawal, a fourth may pay interest only on the minimum account balance, and still others may pay interest quarterly according to a formula.

Third, institutions vary in fees charged for NOWs. Some may provide free checking, others may provide a minimum number of free checks, still others may require per-check fees along with deposit fees. These fees are usually higher than for regular checking accounts, or they might be based upon another deposit requirement—for instance, NOW account fees might be dismissed for depositors who have savings accounts with the institution.

In short, NOW accounts offer the advantage of paying interest on checking balances that might otherwise be fallow. Their disadvantages lie in divergent ways of paying interest, in requiring minimums that might be more lucrative elsewhere, and in charging fees that might effectively eat up all interest paid. Strictly speaking, NOWs are neither savings nor investments; they are *transactions balances*; that is, cash awaiting use.

SAVINGS ACCOUNTS

In addition to providing NOW accounts, nearly all depository institutions offer some form of *basic savings account*. These deposits, too, are loans to the institutions, which pay interest to the depositor/lender.

Commercial banks and S&Ls offer passbook accounts, so-called because of past requirements for the depositor to bring a bankbook to the teller's window when making deposits or withdrawals. Credit unions offer basic *share accounts*, named because depositors hold "shares" in the institution. These shares are not the same as shares of stock in a corporation; they're more akin to "share" in "share and share alike."

A special note about credit unions: credit unions serve only their members, and their members are people who have a common affiliation. To join a credit union you must belong to the group the credit union serves. Universities and corporations frequently have affiliated credit unions, as do military bases, labor unions, trade organizations, and sometimes even neighborhoods.

Basic savings accounts have many names—Christmas Club, Citizens' Accounts, or something mirroring the institution such as AmeriFirst Savings Deposits. However, they are similar in that all require small initial deposits (usually $5), impose equally modest subsequent deposit minimums, have no minimum deposit period, are readily accessible for withdrawal, and are *guaranteed* against loss by a governing state or federal agency. Although it's unlikely they would do so, depositaries can require notice of intention to make withdrawals.

Virtually everyone has had a basic savings account. They are enormously handy. As Christy and Clendenin put it:

> Because these savings-type accounts can be handled personally at a teller's window in transactions of any desired size, they have long been the provence of the small investor. They provide him the opportunity for small investments, the convenience of an emergency financial reserve, a persuasive credit reference, and a ready introduction to a loan source when he desires to purchase real estate or an automobile.[1]

As of 1987, basic savings accounts pay about 5½ percent annual interest, although S&Ls and credit union accounts often pay more, sometimes up to 7 percent. A further peculiarity about credit unions: they call interest payments *dividends*, even though they're interest.

---

[1]George A. Christy and John C. Clendenin, *Introduction to Investments* (New York: McGraw-Hill, 1974).

Two of the most important aspects of savings accounts are their compounding periods and their date of deposit credit. Compounding refers to the frequency with which interest is credited to the savings account. For instance, one commercial bank may pay 5½ percent yearly interest compounded monthly, and its rival across the street may pay 5½ percent yearly interest compounded daily. The more frequent the compounding, the greater the interest received, because compounding results in the payment of interest on interest paid.

Both banks pay a 5½ percent nominal interest rate. Computing the effects of compounding results in a figure called the *effective* interest rate. In this case, the nominal 5½ percent rate becomes a 5.6536 percent effective rate when interest is compounded daily. Most depository institutions advertise their effective rate of interest, so you don't have to compute it. Other things equal, the best savings account is one which pays the highest interest with the most frequent compounding.

Next to effective interest rate, the most important consideration of a standard savings account is the date on which deposits are credited for purposes of paying interest. Years ago, you probably heard the local commercial bank advertise "Save by the tenth and earn from the first." You were being told that the bank credited deposits made up to the 10th day of the month as if they had been made on the 1st day of the month. Between the lines you were also being told that deposits made after the 10th day wouldn't receive interest until the following month. In other words, the bank credited savings deposits on the first of each month, and deposits made after the 10th wouldn't earn interest for 20 days.

Because of competition from other financial institutions, it's common for most depositaries to pay savings account interest from the day of deposit to the day of withdrawal. However, credit unions are still notorious for rules on crediting deposits for payment of interest, and tardy depositors may have money lying for weeks before it starts to earn interest. Further, credit unions often have unusual rules about withdrawals. Many declare that withdrawals will be presumed to come from the earliest deposits, a presumption that cuts into compounding of interest.

Although uniformity is the rule on basic savings accounts

exceptions linger. Some depository institutions still pay interest on average balances, just as some still observe deposit deadlines.

TIME DEPOSIT AND CERTIFICATES

In addition to conventional savings accounts, depository institutions offer *time deposits* or *time certificates.* Time deposits are contractual deposits in which you promise to leave money with the bank, S&L, or credit union for a specified period, ranging from a month to 10 years. Time deposits pay higher interest than savings accounts, the rate increasing with time. A 30-day time deposit may pay 5¾ percent annual interest; a 90-day deposit, 6 percent; a one-year deposit, 7 percent, and so on.

As was true of savings accounts, time deposits are often called something catchy, like *savings certificates* or *passbook plus accounts,* but they hold several common characteristics.

The first is that minimum deposits range from $500 to $5,000, unlike conventional savings accounts that require $1 or $5 minimums.

Second, time deposits need not be purchased in even multiples of the minimum deposit, but once the account is established you usually can't add to it until the time deposit matures (i.e., you can put $510 into a $500 time deposit, but generally you can't open a time deposit for $500 and add $10 the next day).

Third, time deposits have a stated maturity, which is to say they pay a specified rate of interest for a specified period, after which the deposit reverts to a normal savings account or is renewed—*rolled over,* as they say in bankerese. There is also the problem that your banker may roll your account over without telling you. So if you were planning to withdraw a time deposit and you missed the maturity date, you might not be able to get at your money until the new time deposit expires.

Fourth, time deposits are not immediately liquid; if you need your deposit before maturity, you may be out of luck, and even a warmhearted banker will impose "interest penalties for early withdrawal" if you do get your money.

Time deposits are a good way to squeeze a bit more interest

from your bank if you can have cash tied up. Like conventional savings accounts, they are backed by a supervisory agency. The general wording is something like, "Insured up to $100,000 by the Federal Deposit Insurance Corporation, an agency of the Federal Government." For S&Ls, the Federal Savings and Loan Insurance Corporation (FSLIC) is the guarantor, and for credit unions another agency with its set of initials is the backer.

Time deposits or time certificates must not be confused with *certificates of deposit*, or CDs. Certificates of deposit *are* time certificates (specified amount of deposit for a specified time), except they involve higher minimums, usually $1,000 and often $10,000 to $1 million. Larger denomination CDs, those of $100,000 or more, are called *Jumbos*, and those of even larger amounts are often negotiable in that they are bought and sold by money center banks (the multibillion-dollar national and international institutions). Investors with fewer than $5,000 can also buy certificates of deposit indirectly through money market funds, as we'll learn in Chapter Nine.

A new type of CD called a *zero coupon certificate of deposit* is available in minimums of $250, and we'll discuss them in Chapter Ten when we learn about individual retirement accounts (IRAs) for which zero CDs are better suited. We should, however, be aware of the difference between time deposits and certificates of deposit if for no other reason than not to be confused when reading literature from the bank.

MONEY MARKET ACCOUNTS

In addition to NOWs, conventional savings, and time deposits, depository institutions offer *money market accounts* with returns similar to government securities or short-term commercial borrowings. Sometimes interest rates will be "guaranteed" for a specified period—a week to six months—after which they float up or down with prevailing rates, and other times they will bob with the ebb and flow of general financial markets from the day of deposit.

These money market accounts usually require $2,500 minimum deposits. Sometimes they are separate accounts, and sometimes they are tied with NOWs or other checking and savings accounts. Sometimes deposits must be maintained for a specified time, and in other cases not. They may be accompanied by special features, such as checking privileges, free MasterCard and VISA, free travelers cheques, overdraft protection, preapproved lines of credit, or personalized banking services.

The advantages to money market accounts are their higher interest and, for investors who need them, the ancillary services. Disadvantages include higher minimum deposit requirements and other special conditions imposed by the offering institution. Those conditions might include minimum account balances, maintenance fees, restrictions on number of free checks, or higher charges for checks. In addition, methods of computing interest on money market accounts that are tied into special services are far from uniform.

IRAs

Banks, S&Ls, and credit unions also offer *individual retirement accounts* (IRAs). An IRA is a tax-advantaged investment established by Congress to encourage people to plan for retirement. They are important parts of a long-term investment program, and we've reserved a special chapter for them. For the most part, IRAs offered by depository institutions are time deposit accounts with a special annotation on a computer tape.

Interest paid by NOWs, conventional savings, and time deposits is taxable as ordinary income in the year received.

SUMMARY

Now it's time to conclude the chapter on depositaries with a summary of investment advantages and disadvantages.

The advantage to NOW accounts is ability to earn interest on money awaiting other uses, unlike conventional checking accounts. NOW accounts offer immediate liquidity and safety against market risk. Disadvantages are occasionally higher fees than otherwise imposed on checking accounts.

Savings accounts and share accounts with credit unions offer the advantages of being easy to open: no fees to open or maintain an account are charged, initial deposits are small, additional deposits can be made at any time and in any amount, investors often are insured against loss of principal and interest by federal or state agencies, and the deposit never matures. They also provide liquidity, collateral for loans, and advantages from a relationship with a financial institution.

The chief disadvantages of conventional savings accounts are the sometimes obscure way in which interest and deposits are credited and the possibility that other types of accounts may pay higher returns.

Time deposits offer the same advantages of conventional savings accounts plus they pay higher rates of interest, increasing with amount deposited and length of time involved. Their chief disadvantages are higher minimum deposits, inaccessibility of funds prior to maturity, and inability to add to deposits before maturity.

Money market accounts provide all the advantages of other savings vehicles as well as frequently higher interest. Again, disadvantages include higher minimums, occasional fees, and obscure methods of computing interest.

CHAPTER FIVE

Direct Personal Ownership of Common and Preferred Stocks

COMMON STOCKS

Common stocks (also called shares and equities) represent ownership interest in the corporation issuing them. In buying stocks you become an owner of a corporation.

Most investors become stockholders by purchasing shares through stock exchanges. The best-known exchanges are The New York Stock Exchange, called *the big board*, and The American Stock Exchange, called *the curb*. But there are many regional exchanges (Chicago, Baltimore, Cincinnati, Philadelphia) as well as other markets, the most prominent being the over-the-counter market (the OTC).

Exchanges bring sellers of shares into contact with buyers in an orderly market. Sometimes the exchange is in one place, like the NYSE, a Gothic building in New York, and sometimes the "exchange" is scattered, like the OTC, which is thousands of market-makers transacting stocks from computer terminals. Either arrangement permits strangers to conduct business (potentially with mutual profit) quickly and efficiently under terms regulating all transactions. In short, exchanges provide liquidity. You access this system through fee-charging middlemen—stockbrokers—who are agents for parties conducting transactions.

The day's security transactions are published in *The Wall Street Journal* and local newspapers' business sections. Let's say you're considering becoming an owner of American Telephone and Telegraph. You open the paper to quotations from the New York Stock Exchange, because that's where AT&T is traded. Under column A you find:

27⅞ 21⅝ ATT 1.20 11 17545 25⅜ 22 23⅜ +⅛

Stock prices appear as fractions that must be converted to decimals representing dollars and cents, which in turn are multiplied by the number of shares to be purchased or sold.

The first two numbers reveal the 52-week trading range of the stock. AT&T traded at a yearly high of 27⅞, which becomes 27.875, or $27.88 per share. The minimum value of one share during the preceeding 52 weeks was 21⅝, which becomes 21.625, or $21.63. One hundred shares of AT&T stock fluctuated between $2,787.50 and $2,162.50. Compute figures for 5, 9, or 12 shares by multiplying price per share times number of shares.

Most stock prices are measured in units of ⅛, called a *bit*, which is 12.5 cents (⅛ = .125, which is .125 of $1, or 12.5 cents). However, low-priced or infrequently traded stocks are tracked in ¹⁄₁₆ths (6.25 cents) or ¹⁄₃₂ds (3.125 cents). If a stock is quoted at 1¹⁄₁₆, its price is $1.0625 per share. One hundred shares would be worth $106.25. Five shares would be worth $5.3125. Twenty-seven shares would be worth_____? If you answered $28.6875 you are following well.

The third item in the newspaper ledger is the name of the stock, American Telephone and Telegraph. Elsewhere under the A column we find AtlRich, or Atlantic Richfield, and AldSgnl or Allied-Signal Inc. Abbreviations conserve space.

The next entry is 1.20, which reveals AT&T pays a dividend of $1.20 per share per year. Multiply $1.20 times the number of shares to derive the dividends received from a given investment. Buy 10 shares, and you'll receive $12 in yearly dividends. Dividends are important, and we'll talk about them in a moment.

The next item, 11, is the price-earnings ratio, called PE or PE ratio and occasionally the times earnings ratio or times earnings. The PE ratio is determined by dividing the price of a stock by its most recent yearly earnings. AT&T is selling at 11 times its earnings. In other words, the buyer pays $11 for every $1 of earnings reported.

The next item, 17545, tells the number of shares changing hands during the trading day. Usually the number represents sales volume in hundreds. In this case, 1,754,500 shares changed hands on a single day.

The next two entries reveal the daily trading range of the stock. In this case, the numbers are 25⅜ and 22, meaning the stock's daily high was $25.375 and its low was $22 even.

The next number is the closing price. In this case, the final trade of the day in AT&T was $23.375. Some financial pages note the opening price of the stock, usually printed immediately after daily volume.

The final number is +⅛, meaning the stock closed 12.5 cents higher today than the previous day. Had the number been −⅛ the closing price of 23⅜ would have been 12.5 cents less than the previous day's close. If closing price were unchanged from the day earlier, the final item would have been an ellipsis (. . .).

Quotations for stocks traded over the counter are recorded differently. Here's the entry for Quixote Corporation:

Quixote Corp.   48   16   16½   ...

The first entry names the corporation. No entry identifies a dividend because the stock pays none.

The next entry is trading volume, meaning 4,800 shares traded hands.

The next two items, 16 and 16½ are not daily high and low prices, as with AT&T and stocks on the New York or American Exchanges. Instead, they are bid and asked prices established by the dealers in this stock.

As we noted, OTC markets are electronic networks of specialists who buy and sell a stock. The person trading Quixote is willing to buy shares at a price of $16 per share. This is the *bid price*. The dealer bids that price to purchase the securities. The *asked price* is the price the dealer asks in making securities for sale. In this example, the dealer is asking 16½ per share (16.5 or $16.50) to sell shares of Quixote.

Bid and asked prices are quoted from the vantage of dealers. The dealer pays the bid price to buy and receives the asked price when selling. Your figures are reversed. You pay asked prices to buy and receive bid prices to sell.

The ellipsis (. . .) indicates the *bid* price is unchanged from the previous day. Had the quotation read +¼, for example, the bid price would be .25 (25 cents) higher than yesterday's bid. In other words, the dealer raised by 25 cents the price bid (willing to purchase) for stock, which means the price you'd receive for selling increased 25 cents.

COMMON STOCKS AND INCOME

Common stocks offer capital gains, also called *capital appreciation*. If you recall Chapter One, a capital gain is the difference between purchase price and selling price. Sell stocks for more than you paid, and you have a capital gain.

Capital gains come into being because investors buy stocks they believe will increase in price. Sure enough, as they buy, prices increase. In other words, investors drive up prices of stocks in anticipation that stocks will increase in price.

The concept of capital gains is expressed as *capital growth* and institutionalized in *aggressive capital gains* and *long-term growth*. The former category includes stocks that increase rapidly in price, and pursuit of aggressive capital gains is the chasing after of stocks which promise quick price increases. Long-term capital gains belong to stocks that increase gradually in price, keeping pace with their industries or the general economy.

In addition to capital gains, many common stocks pay dividends. Again: a dividend is a payment from earnings by a corporation to its owners. Stocks noted for generous dividends are called income stocks, and investors attracted to them are called income investors.

Nothing demands the board of directors to pay a dividend. Quixote Corporation paid none. Further, the board can omit or reduce dividends. However, corporations are reluctant to reduce or omit dividends, and many have histories of regular dividend increases. Also, corporations may pay "special dividends" on a one-time-only basis. The board of AT&T could decide that business has been so great that a special dividend of, say, 10 cents per share is warranted.

Besides cash dividends, corporations may declare *stock dividends* and, rarely, may pay dividends in merchandise. Stock dividends are paid by issuing additional stock to every shareholder prorated according to number of shares owned, instead of or in addition to a cash dividend.

Don't confuse stock dividends with *stock splits*. A stock dividend is the issuance of additional shares. A stock split is the multiplication of a corporation's stock into a larger number of shares. Say, for example, that a corporation has 1 million shares selling at $50 per share and declares a two-for-one split. If approved by shareholders, the split would result in the company's having 2 million shares, and each shareholder would receive double the number of shares he or she currently owns. The price of each share would likely fall to $25, reflecting the doubling of shares.

Merchandise dividends are rare. As an example, Procter and Gamble could mail every shareholder a box of Tide as a dividend.

Even though stock quotations reveal yearly dividends, corporations pay dividends quarterly on a date announced in advance. Dividend announcements usually read something like "The Board of Directors of Granny's Grits announces a 10 percent increase in the Company's quarterly dividend to 66 cents per share from 60 cents, payable on March 1 to holders of record on February 15."

Dividend announcements contain three important bits of information: amount of the dividend and increase, the record date by which you must own stock to receive dividends, and the date it will be paid. If you buy a share of Granny's Grits by February 15, you will be entitled—and "entitled" is accurate in this case—to a dividend of 66 cents on March 1. If you buy after February 15, you don't receive the dividend, and if you sell your shares of Granny's Grits before February 15 you'll not receive a dividend.

DIVIDENDS VERSUS CAPITAL GAINS

Whether investors should prefer income from dividends or capital gains is hotly debated. Some investors want dividends, and other investors want corporations to reinvest earnings for higher profits and share prices.

Investors favoring capital gains argue that they are the best way to make the most money from stocks. In addition, capital gains are said to keep investors ahead of inflation better than dividends. Another advantage to capital gains, as of 1987 at least, is that capital gains aren't taxed until you sell stock that's grown in price.

Investors favoring dividends argue the following:

1. It's easy to pick dividend-paying stocks. It is not so easy to pick stock that will appreciate.
2. Dividends can be used for expenses or for other kinds of investments while not interrupting the source of income. Capital gains are cash only when you sell stock.
3. Dividend yields are easily calculated, and, therefore, can be compared easily to yields from competing investments. Dividend yield is the dividend divided by purchase price of the stock. If AT&T is paying $1.20 and you buy at $25 per share, your yield is 4.8 percent ($1.20 divided by $25). That yield will be yours as long as you own AT&T and as long as it pays dividends. If AT&T increases its dividend, your yield increases.

However, let's not forget disadvantages of common stocks.

1. Picking stocks is a trying task for professionals, much less beginners.
2. Investors who have less than $5,000 won't be able to diversify holdings.
3. Stock prices fall as well as rise.
4. Commissions eat into investment capital, especially as a percentage of cash invested, and they apply to purchases and sales. Therefore, if commissions are $50 for purchase and sale, "round trip commissions" are $100. One hundred shares have to rise one point before you break even. In addition, stock purchases involve transactions taxes levied by cities where exchanges are located. There's also something called an *odd lot differential.*

Any stock purchase that is not an even multiple of 100 shares is an odd lot. You must pay an additional 12.5 cents per share to buy an odd lot. If you buy 100 shares of AT&T at $25 per share, you pay $2,500 ($25 × 100). If you buy 99 shares, you pay $2,487.38 instead of $2,475.

The same holds true of selling odd lots—a sacrifice of

12.5 cents per share. If you sell 100 shares of AT&T at $25 per share, you receive $2,500. If you sell 99 shares, you receive $2,462.63—not $2,475.

PREFERRED STOCKS

Common stocks, the basic ownership interest, aren't the only stock issued by corporations. Another often issued and widely held is *preferred stock*. Like common stock, preferreds offer opportunity for capital gains and dividends. However, should a corporation declare bankruptcy, owners of preferred stocks receive liquidated assets before owners of common stock receive anything. This is the origin of the term *preferred stock*, and it indicates "preferred over common in claims on corporate assets." In general, though, the advantage of preferred is that preferred stock dividends must be paid before common stock dividends.

Preferred stocks pay dividends at a fixed rate, whereas dividends on common stocks are or can be raised by the board. This is an advantage and disadvantage. The advantage is that the preferred dividend, assuming the company isn't going bankrupt, won't be lowered. On the other hand, it won't likely be raised.

Most preferreds are *cumulative*. Should a corporation defer paying a cumulative preferred dividend, that dividend accumulates. All deferred and current preferred dividends must be paid before dividends on common stock.

Deferred dividends belong to the current owner of the preferred and not to whomever owned the stock while dividends were deferred. If you were the hapless owner of Digital Datadump series A Cumulative Preferred, which hasn't paid a dividend in 10 years, your patience won't be rewarded if you sell before the dividend is declared. All 10 years' of accumulated dividends will go to whomever bought the stock you sold, even though he or she owned it 24 hours and you owned it 10 years.

Participating preferreds "participate" in the corporation's success via additional, special, or extra dividends if business is especially profitable—and, of course, they'll also increase in price with increased corporate profitability.

Variable rate preferreds pay dividends that vary. Some, for instance, pay dividends tied to T-bill interest rates. Others pay a base dividend with increments tied to the corporation's profitability and are similar to participating preferred. Still others offer a minimum and maximum payment, with variances determined by formula.

Convertible preferreds can be converted into other securities, usually common stock of the corporation, at the owners' discretion. Terms of issue will specify that, say, five shares of preferred may be converted into one share of common stock. This provision allows preferred to participate in the company's good fortune, so its price will rise as the common stock rises.

Most preferreds are *callable*. "Call provisions" permit corporations to buy back part or all of a series of preferred at an established price after a specified date. Usually the call price is the preferred's *par value*, an amount specified by the issuing corporation that allegedly measures what the preferred is "worth." Par value places a theoretical ceiling upon the price to which the preferred can rise. If the corporation can call preferred at par, investors won't pay more than par for preferred, other things being equal.

(If a preferred is convertible into common, it may sell above call price, reflecting investors' option of converting preferred into common. In the case of convertibles, the price ceiling is call price or conversion price.)

At this point you've come to expect a summary, but we're not through discussing the kinds of corporate securities investors can purchase directly. So we'll delay our summary of stocks until the next chapter, which discusses corporate bonds.

CHAPTER SIX

Direct Personal Ownership of Corporate Bonds

After "buy low, sell high," the best-known investment homily was uttered by Polonius, a character in *Hamlet* who advised, "Neither a borrower nor a lender be." Polonius was no bond trader.

Stocks are equity investments, and whoever owns stocks owns a portion of the corporation issuing them. Corporate bonds are creditor investments, and whoever owns them holds the issuing corporation's IOU. Lenders expect not only repayment of the loan (principal), but also returns for risks of lending and rewards for postponing consumption. That compensation is provided by payment of interest.

BOND INTEREST

Unlike stockholder-owners, who share in profits from the corporation, bondholder-lenders are entitled to return of principal plus stated interest payments and nothing else. In strict financial definition, corporate bonds are backed by collateral, usually cash or salable equipment. Most corporations issue *debentures* backed only by the corporation's obligation to pay interest and repay principal. For a live corporation, bonds and debentures are binding arrangements—interest and principal must be paid—so we needn't be fussy about the distinction. But if a corporation goes under, the distinction can be important.

Bonds are a corporation's senior security. Debentures are

junior to bonds (in fact, some debentures are junior to other debentures) and senior to preferred stock. If the corporation goes under, bondholders and other debtors have first claim on liquidated assets, followed by holders of debentures, preferred stock, and common stock in that order. This hierarchy understood, we'll call all corporate IOUs "bonds" for convenience.

Corporate bonds have five features: issuer, maturity date, coupon rate, par value, and price. Like stocks, bonds are traded on exchanges, and trades are reported in the financial press. To pick an example, open the financial section to the page headed "New York Exchange Bonds," look under the column of "A's," and you'll locate

ATT   7⅛s03   11   140   68   67⅜   67½   +½

This is a bond issued by American Telephone and Telegraph. We know that because the first item names the issuer. The other numbers resemble stock quotations, but similarities end with resemblance.

The second entry, 7⅛s03, bears two items of information. The 7⅛ is the bond's coupon, and the 03 tells the bond's maturity date.

The coupon, or coupon payment rate, is the amount of yearly interest paid by this bond. It is represented by numerals and fractions that must be converted to decimals and multiplied by 10. Here we have 7⅛, which converts to 7.125. Multiplying by 10 gives 71.25. Add a dollar sign, and the enigma is translated into $71.25.

The coupon rate of this bond is $71.25. Each bond pays $71.25 per year in interest. Corporate bonds pay semiannual interest, meaning the owner receives half the stated coupon rate every six months. In this case, a check for $35.62 would arrive in the mail every six months.

Payments last until the bond is sold or matures, which brings us to the second part of 7⅛s03—the 03. That pair of numerals reveals this bond matures in 2003. Had the entry read 91, the bond would mature in 1991; 89, in 1989; 17, in 2017.

A rare exception: some bonds pay varying rates, just as some preferreds pay variable dividends. In these rare cases, interest payments may be determined by profitability of the issuer or by indexes to inflation or yields on other securities.

A rarer exception: some bonds never mature. They're annotated perp for *perpetuities* (as with in perpetuity) where otherwise would be numerals indicating maturity. Also called consols, these bonds have no face value, and they're sold at prices dictated by the market.

On the maturity date, the issuer makes final payment of semiannual interest and repays the principal. That's where par value comes in. Par value—also called denomination, face value, or maturity value—is the amount the bond will be worth upon maturity. Nearly all corporate bonds have a par of $1,000. That is the amount of the corporation's indebtedness to the holder of one bond.

The next item, 11, is the bond's current yield, or the coupon rate divided by the selling price of the bond.

Following the current yield is the number of bonds exchanged on that trading day. Unlike stocks, bond trades aren't reported in hundreds, so 140 ATT 7⅛s03 were sold.

The next three numbers are referred to as the high-low-close: the daily high price (68), the daily low (67⅜), and the day's closing price (67½). These prices are implied multiples of 10, differing from stock quotes. The price of 68 is $680; 67½ is $675.00. A corporate bond's price is determined by converting fractions to decimals and multiplying by 10, just as the dollar amount of the coupon is determined by converting fractions to decimals and multiplying by 10.

BONDS AND THE OPEN MARKET

The astute reader will sense something discomforting about the price of this bond. A corporate bond's par value—the indebtedness to the bond's owner—is $1,000. Yet this bond can be bought for $680. To explain this $320 discrepancy, we have to distinguish between bonds bought when issued and when bought on the open market of the public exchange.

Bonds are usually offered to the public at or near par value, excepting zero coupon bonds that we'll discuss in a moment. You pay $1,000 now, and you get back $1,000 upon maturity. During the interim, you collect interest. The interest is a stated percentage of par value, say 5 percent, and that translates easily enough into $50 a year ($1,000 × 0.05 = $50). If things stayed that way, bonds would be simple. Obviously, things changed.

People sell bonds as needs for cash or desires for other

investments change. Like all sellers, they receive what the market will pay. Frequently the market—that is, other people—won't pay the same price as the original buyer.

One reason why people may not be willing to pay $1,000 for a bond is changed creditworthiness of the issuer. Another reason why bonds don't always trade at par is that the general level of interest rates changes, and with changes in interest rates come changes in prices of traded bonds.

Now for an illustration of those two points. We'll assume that the general level of interest rates doesn't change but creditworthiness of the issuer does.

Let's say a buggy whip manufacturer issues a bond at par with a coupon of 5 percent when issuers of similar creditworthiness and the general level of interest rates dictate that 5 percent is a competitive rate. People pay $1,000 for the bond, and they receive $50 per year.

However, after the bond was issued along come Henry Ford and the automobile. Neither event portends well for makers of buggy whips, and owners of the bonds want to sell. Potential buyers of the bonds also realize that creditworthiness of buggy whip makers has slipped, so they won't pay $1,000 to sellers. Sellers will have to accept the revised market-established price for the bonds, and that price will reflect expectations for the future of buggy whip makers.

Say the marketplace reevaluates these bonds at $500. The initial owner can sell this bond at $500, losing half his investment, or hold it and hope the buggy whip company won't go bankrupt before the bonds mature.

Under these circumstances, who would buy the bonds? Investors who believe fears about the automobile are overstated and investors willing to accept a higher return offered by the depressed bond price. Remember, features of the bond haven't changed. The issuer must pay $50 per year and is obligated to repay the $1,000 borrowed.

However, because the price of the bond has been depressed, the rate of return is higher. The new purchaser still receives $50 per year, but he pays only $500—the new market price—for that yearly income instead of $1,000. The new owner receives a 10 percent current yield instead of 5 percent ($50 divided by $500 instead of $50 divided by $1,000). In addition, the new purchaser still holds a claim on $1,000. When the bond matures, the new purchaser receives the $1,000 that would have gone to the original purchaser.

The same opportunity arises when the general level of interest rates changes. Interest rates rise and fall for many reasons, and prices of bonds move inversely to interest rates. As interest rates rise, bond prices fall; as interest rates fall, bond prices rise. Now we'll return to our example, but with a different scenario.

We still have the buggy whip company and its bonds paying 5 percent, or $50 per year, for which investors paid $1,000 at initial issue. Those terms were, as we said, competitive for firms of similar creditworthiness under prevailing general rates of interest. Five years later, however, general interest rates, which were 5 percent, are now 10 percent. The investor with $1,000 can invest at 10 percent, receiving $100 yearly ($100 is 10 percent of $1,000). What happens to the price of buggy whip bonds? Again it will fall to $500.

The reasoning leading to that answer is provided by provisions of the bond. Remember, the bond was issued at 5 percent and pays $50 yearly. With interest rates at 10 percent, what would an investor have to spend in order to receive $50 per year? The answer: $500. At prevailing rates of 10 percent, investors won't pay $1,000 to receive $50—half what they could be earning elsewhere. For the buggy whip bond to be competitive in public markets it will have to increase payments to 10 percent, or the price will have to fall so that $50 yearly interest payments are competitive with other investments.

The issuer has no incentive to increase interest payments. That means the price of the bond has to fall until a payment of $50 is competitive in an economy that established 10 percent as the going rate. So we ask, "$50 is 10 percent of what amount?" Again, $500.

Who loses? The buyer who paid $1,000 for the bond. Financial markets have decided this investment is now worth only $500. Who wins? The new buyer who still receives $50 a year but who pays only $500 for that income. The new buyer receives a 10 percent current yield and still has $1,000 coming from this issuer.

We can now see why the AT&T bond is selling for $680 instead of $1,000. The coupon rate of $71.25 ceased to represent a market-level return as general interest rates rose. Because investors want to maximize income, they were no longer willing to pay $1,000 for payments of $71.25. The price, accordingly, fell as owners of the bond sold to reinvest at higher rates of interest and as new purchasers refused to accept old rates of interest. The $320 disappeared for old owners of the bond, and it will reappear in checkbooks of new owners when the bond matures in 2003.

Of course, a great deal can happen between 1987 and 2003. For one thing, the general level of interest rates can fall. Remembering that bond prices move inversely to interest rates, what do we predict for the price of the AT&T bond? It will rise. To illustrate that, we return to the buggy whip bond.

When we left our forlorn bond it was still paying $50 per year and selling at $500—half par value—because general interest rates had risen from 5 percent to 10 percent. Slowly, however, financial circumstances change, and interest rates fall from 10 percent to 9, to 8, all the way back to 5 percent. Suddenly, there's new life for the old buggy whip bonds.

Investors are looking for something to invest in. Their collective eye traces the B column on the bond pages of the newspaper, where they find Buggy Whips, Inc., selling at $500 with a coupon of $50 per year for a yield of 10 percent. While other investments offer 5 percent, here's a hot number yielding 10 percent.

They call their brokers, buy one—or 7, 10, or 91—buggy whip bonds, and secure a 10 percent yield. Before long, others discover buggy whip bonds are paying more than the prevailing rate, and they, income maximizers all, start buying the bonds. Lazarus-like, the price of the bonds rises from the dead. Those who bought the bonds at $500 aren't going to sell at $500 because they're earning 10 percent interest ($50 coupon divided by $500 purchase price) while everyone else is earning 5 percent. So potential buyers have to pay more to induce owners to part with the bonds.

Eventually, buyers will have to pay the full $1,000 if they want the buggy whip bonds. At that point, the bonds will be yielding the market rate of 5 percent ($50 divided by $1,000), and they'll have to compete equally with other investments paying 5 percent. Those who bought the bonds at $1,000 have broken even, but those who bought at $500 have doubled their money.

Through increases in interest rates and corresponding decreases in bond prices investors—like those who bought the buggy whip bonds at $500—can purchase bonds at *discounts from par.* Corporate bonds selling at around $750 are *deep discount bonds.* Availability of bonds at prices below par adds a new income dimension to bonds: capital appreciation.

Recall that capital appreciation results from selling at a price greater than initial payment. That happens when you pay $500 for a bond maturing at $1,000, but, as with the second buggy whip example, it also happens any time bond prices rise.

Therefore, just as total return from stocks is comprised of dividends plus capital appreciation, total return from bonds is comprised of interest payments plus capital appreciation. Interest payments are taxed as current income, and so, under 1987 tax law, are capital gains from bonds.

YIELD ON BONDS

We've already mentioned two types of yield from bonds. Nominal yield is the percentage relationship of the coupon rate to the face value of the bond, nearly always $1,000. For our buggy whip bonds, nominal yield was 5 percent (5 percent of $1,000 face value).

The second type of yield was current yield, or annual interest payment divided by selling price. In our buggy whip bond, we saw that current yield fluctuated from 5 percent to 10 percent ($50 divided by $1,000 and $50 divided by $500).

But the investor who buys a bond at a discount and plans to keep it until maturity is interested in *yield to maturity,* the percentage the average annual gain bears to average annual investment.

Average annual gain is interest payments plus capital appreciation. Average annual investment is the midpoint between buyer's cost and maturity value. That's the easy explanation, but there is a formula which makes everyone who understands it feel smart:

$$\frac{C + \dfrac{D}{YTM}}{\dfrac{PP + PV}{2}}$$

The C is the yearly coupon payment. D is the bond's discount from par. YTM is years to maturity. PP is purchase price, and PV is the bond's par value. The 2 is necessary to make everything average. The numerator reveals average annual gain, which is interest payments plus capital appreciation. The denominator is average annual investment, the midpoint between purchase price and par value. The resulting figure is the yield to maturity, the total yield received by the holder of the bond.

We'll look at yield to maturity of our buggy whips. We'll assume they mature in 10 years and that we buy them at $500 5 years before maturity. The coupon payment remains $50 yearly. Figures enter the formula:

$$\frac{\$50 + \dfrac{\$500}{5}}{\dfrac{\$500 + \$1,000}{2}}$$

Mathematical wizardry reveals:

$$\frac{\$50 + \$100}{\$750}$$

which breaks down to

$$\frac{\$150}{\$750}$$

which gives a yield to maturity of .200, an even 20 percent. In other words, whoever purchases the bond at $500 and holds it until maturity receives a yield to maturity of 20 percent.

A similar figure is *yield to call.* Some bonds are callable just like some preferred stocks. (Similarly, some bonds are convertible.) The bond covenant will specify call price and date of eligibility for redemption. Yield to call is computed like yield to maturity, substituting call price for par value and number of years until redemption for years to maturity. Obviously, bonds provide different yields, and the pertinent yield is the one coinciding with the investor's intention to hold or sell.

Just as bonds may sell at discounts, they occasionally sell at *premiums,* meaning a bond with $1,000 face value may sell for more than $1,000. This situation occurs because corporations floating a bond issue must offer investors competitive yields, and after the issue is sold interest rates fall.

Not long ago, prevailing interest rates exceeded 10 percent, and corporations selling new bonds had to offer that coupon rate. Shortly thereafter, interest rates fell, drawing investors to high-coupon bonds just issued. Prices of those bonds rose to substantially above par until their current yields were bid down to the prevailing rate. Even so, the issuer is obligated to repay only the $1,000 loan represented by the bond, so whoever buys bonds selling at premiums takes a loss eventually.

Losses from buying bonds at a premium may not be declared on federal income tax. As you might expect, investors who buy a bond at par and find it selling at a premium do have to declare a capital gain if they sell.

ZERO COUPON BONDS

Some bonds that appear to offer capital appreciation don't. Such is the case with *zero coupon bonds*. Zeros pay no coupon interest. Instead, they are sold at extremely deep discounts, and they mature at par on maturity. The difference between purchase price and par value, nearly always $1,000, is accrued interest.

Here's a quotation for a zero:

Bkam   zr93s   ...   136   58¼   58   58¼   −⅛

As with conventional corporates, the first item names the issuer, Bank of America. The zr identifies the issue as a zero, and 93 is the maturity date of 1993. The next figure is trading volume, followed by the high-low-close and comparison with the previous day's close, off fractionally.

The item of attraction is price, ranging from $582.50 to $582.00. You buy this bond for $582 and receive $1,000 in 1993. In the interim you receive nothing. There's no current yield or nominal yield. Only yield to maturity applies, and that's calculated from compound interest tables. Yield to maturity is around 8 percent for this bond.

The investor who chiefly profits from zeros is one who puts them into an individual retirement account. We have a chapter devoted to IRAs, and we'll learn that income from an IRA isn't taxed until withdrawn. Therefore, the Internal Revenue Service's demand that you pay tax on income not received doesn't aply to IRAs, and zeros are advisable for that purpose.

For a comprehensive discussion of all types of zero coupon investments, including tax consequences and portfolio strategies, please buy your author's third book, *The Dow Jones-Irwin Guide to Zero Coupon Investments*.[1] Its reviewers have called it the most informative treatment of zeros available, and it lists where to buy them and what to look for in features and advantages.

BOND OWNERSHIP

The investor contemplating personal ownership of corporate bonds must consider several circumstances.

First, bonds are purchased and sold through stockbrokers, who charge commissions for transactions. In addition, bonds pay interest semiannually, and whoever buys a bond between interest payments must pay the seller the amount of prorated interest. The quoted price of bonds doesn't include interim interest.

Second, the buyer must be aware of the issuer's solvency. Buyers are aided by rating services who gauge a corporation's reliability by affixing a rating to it. Usually, ratings are AAA, AA, A, BBB, BB, B, CCC, CC, C, and D. The range reflects estimated ability of issuers to meet their obligations, with AAA issuers carrying the highest and D (in default) the lowest.

Third, buyers must select maturities carefully. Long-running bonds offer attractive yields, but their prices fluctuate severely with interest rates. Bonds with closer maturities yield less, but prices are more stable.

Fourth, buyers must be aware they are purchasing a fixed-income stream of interest payments and capital appreciation. Whenever investors commit to a fixed-income security, they must be aware that interest income will not increase.

---

[1]Homewood, Ill.: Dow Jones-Irwin, 1986.

What are advantages of bond ownership?

First, investors are "guaranteed" interest payments and a return of principal. Or at least they're in line for whatever is left if a corporation can't meet its obligations.

Second, bond investments generate predictable returns. Barring default, bonds will pay a stated rate of interest and will mature at a known price.

Third, bonds frequently offer compelling current yields and yields to maturity.

Fourth, some bonds do provide additional attractive features. We mentioned that some are convertible into common or preferred stocks of the issuing corporation, but other issues have more esoteric and potentially attractive features, such as payment in foreign currencies or conversion into precious metals.

SUMMARY

It's time to wrap up corporate investments with a summary and comparison.

Common stocks are the essential ownership interest in a corporation. Whoever owns common stocks owns a portion of the issuing company and participates in rewards of the company's operations. Those rewards come as dividends—quarterly checks to shareholders—and as capital appreciation from the market valuing shares more highly.

Common stocks fluctuate in price, and dividends are not required to be paid. Those are main disadvantages of common stocks.

Preferred stocks also represent ownership in a corporation, but ownership senior to common stocks. If dividends are declared, preferred stockholders must be paid first.

The chief disadvantage of preferreds is that dividends are not obligatory and are rarely increased, although cumulative and variable rate preferreds offset some of that disadvantage. Also, preferreds tend to be more sensitive to interest rate fluctuations than common stocks.

Bonds and debentures are creditor securities, not ownership securities. Bondholders receive semiannual payments of stated interest and a return of principal. Zero coupon bonds pay interest only upon maturity. Unlike common and preferred stock dividends, interest is an obligation of the corporation. Market conditions make possible the purchase of bonds at discounts from par, providing capital gains in addition to interest income.

Bonds are fixed-income investments. Except in special issues, holders don't receive more than interest and repayment of principal. Excepting the rare case of perpetuals, bonds expire on a given date and do not provide returns indefinitely. Increases in the general level of interest rates can depress bond prices significantly. Some bonds and debentures can be called prior to maturity.

With that summary we end our discussion of direct corporate investment. A rather extended discussion of indirect corporate investment lies ahead, but we aren't quite through with bonds yet.

Ownership of Government and Municipal Bonds

Corporate America isn't the only entity raising money in the bond market. In fact, America itself is the biggest borrower of all. The federal government's debt dwarfs the debt of the Fortune 500. When you add to the federal government's debt governmental agency securities, state, municipal, and local bonds, and then add all the money governments will attempt to raise this year alone by selling bonds, the total is staggering.

Although major purchasers of government bonds are institutions, private investors are prominent buyers. Many investors own government securities indirectly through financial intermediaries, but many also are direct owners, for government securities are readily accessible, safe, liquid, and—in some cases—inexpensive, ranging from $25 and $500 for EE and HH savings bonds, $1,000 to $5,000 for notes and bonds, to $10,000 for T-bills. In addition, several financial innovations allow investors to participate in portfolios of governmental securities.

BILLS, NOTES, AND BONDS

A bit of classification is in order. Although corporate IOUs are for the most part bonds or debentures, government debt comes as bills, notes, and bonds.

Treasury *bills* are short-term paper sold in minimums of $10,000 (with additional multiples of $5,000) to mature in three months, six months, and one year. They may be purchased through brokers and commercial banks, which will charge a fee, or without fee from the Federal Reserve or its banks and branches. Because we're working with only $5,000, direct purchase of T-bills is beyond our reach, but they're available if you have the capital.

Uncle Sam issued *notes* to avoid his own regulations. Not long ago a legal ceiling on interest applied to anything the Treasury Department called a *bond*, and prevailing interest rates exceeded that ceiling. Even the government must pay competitive rates for money—interest being the price of money—so the Treasury sold *notes*, claiming notes were exempt from interest restrictions on bonds. This distinction slid by, and U.S. Treasury notes are still with us. Like conventional corporate bonds, notes pay semiannual coupon interest and are initially issued at face value. Notes mature in 1 to 10 years and if purchasing them at initial offering you must usually buy five bonds, each with a face value of $1,000. In resale markets, however, most notes may be purchased singly in $1,000 denominations, although for some the minimum purchase is five bonds.

Treasury *bonds* are like notes except they're issued to mature in longer than 10 years. A favorite of dowagers, trust funds, dynasty builders, foreign governments, and gangsters laundering cash, Treasury bonds are sacred necessities of conservative portfolios. Savings bonds are a subdivision of Treasury bonds, and because they're useful to small investors, we have an extended discussion of them.

The attraction of Treasury bills, notes, and bonds (often simply called USGs) is that they're backed by the full faith and credit of the United States government (hence the term *USG*). Other governments have repudiated debts, but we believe ours won't, so USGs are considered free from default. But like all bonds USGs fluctuate in price (EE and HH bonds excepted), and, like all bonds, USGs are vulnerable to inflation's reducing purchasing power of their fixed-income stream. With a more legitimate claim to financial and semantic accuracy, USGs do represent a risk-free *return*. The issuer has a monopoly on printing dollars, after all, but a risk-free return is not a risk-free investment.

Because they are this planet's closest approximation of

a sure thing, most USGs are excellent collateral (EE and HH bonds excepted), and some—called flower bonds—are accepted at par, regardless of market price, in payment of estate taxes. Because USGs are secure, they typically yield about a percent less than highest-grade corporate bonds. Interest from government securities is exempt from state and municipal income tax.

Buying government bonds and notes directly presents minor problems not encountered with purchases of corporate debt. Not all stockbrokers, especially discount brokers, deal in USGs. In addition, prices of government bonds and notes are quoted differently from corporates.

BOND QUOTATIONS

Like corporates, government bonds and notes are quoted in points. Par equals 100 points—$1,000—making each point worth $10. However, fractions of a point are expressed in 32ds even though they look like decimals. Each 32d is worth 31.25 cents. Fractions pertaining to the coupon rate are quoted in conventional eighths that must be converted to decimals and multiplied by 10, and the current yield is given in decimals that don't need conversion to anything, least of all 32ds. So in reading quotations for USGs what looks like a decimal is really a 32d unless it's actually a decimal, and what looks like a fraction is really a decimal expressed in eighths.

If you think you've got that, later in advanced financial readings you'll encounter *basis points*, which are not the points we're talking about, and some financial pages don't quote USGs that way at all. Anyway, here's a sample:

10⅜s   2007−12   Nov   97.16   97.24   +.26   10.62

USG quotations are isolated in a separate section of the financial pages reserved for government securities, so there's no need to identify the issuer.

The entry, 10⅜s, looks familiar, and it means what we've learned to read it as meaning. It is the coupon rate of this bond—10.375, which is multiplied by 10 to become 103.75, or $103.75. Owners of this bond receive $103.75 yearly in semiannual interest payments.

The 2007-12 is slightly unfamiliar. The 2007 is the year in

which Uncle Sam may call this bond, just as corporate issuers may call some preferreds and bonds. Not all USGs are callable, and no one can remember the U.S. government's ever calling debt, anyway. The −12 represents the year 2012, when this bond matures.

The Nov, which surprisingly means November, reveals two pieces of information about this bond: (1) it matures in November 2012, when final payment of semiannual interest and repayment of principal are due; (2) it makes one semiannual interest payment each November. Because semiannual interest is paid twice yearly, we may deduce this bond also pays interest in May—six months from November. Review of USG quotations reveals that one is maturing virtually every month into the next century.

The next two items, 97.16 and 97.24 are similar to closing bid-and-asked prices of OTC stocks. However, seeming decimals actually mean 32ds, or 31.25 cents. So 97.16 is 97 points plus 16/32 of one point. Each point is worth $10, so the 97 points mean a price of $970. Each 32d is 31.25 cents, and there are 16 of them in the quote, meaning 500 cents or $5. Added together, $970 plus $5 is $975.

Comparing USG quotes with corporate bond quotations, the 97.16 means 97 16/32, which reduces to 97½ and is rendered into the fraction 97.5, becoming $975.

Try deciphering 97.24. You should be able to figure out that the bond's asking price is $977.50. If this issue sells in five-bond minimums, you'll have to pay $4,887.50. Otherwise, you can buy one bond for $977.50.

Fully rendered into English, the bid-and-asked means dealers in these USGs are willing to buy at $975 and sell for $977.50. You pay the dealer's asking price—$977.50—to buy and accept the bid price—$975—to sell.

Four additional words about those prices: (1) the quoted market for USGs is for lots of $1 million, and transactions involving lesser amounts mean lower bid and higher asked prices; (2) prices don't include commissions; (3) prices for USGs change every minute, so any quote is history; (4) the quoted price doesn't include accrued interest you pay the seller if purchasing bonds between interest dates. For any of those reasons, price shown may not be the price you receive or pay.

The next entry—+.26—shows that the closing bid price increased ²⁶⁄₃₂ds over the previous day's closing bid. Considering that ¹⁄₃₂ equals 31.25 cents, we know this dealer was willing to pay $8.125 more for this bond than yesterday (31.25 cents × 26 = 812.5 cents or $8.125).

The final item—10.62—is the current yield (coupon rate divided by current price). That's 10.62 percent—straight out, no hidden ¹⁄₃₂ds or ⅛ths. Other diverting and occasionally important facts about USGs and their quotations:

1.   The annotation, n, beside an issue means it's a note rather than a bond. It doesn't matter whether you buy a Treasury note or a Treasury bond so long as you get the maturity and coupon you want. Both are backed by the United States, and market forces contrive bonds of similar maturity to pay similar current interest.

2.   Government bonds and notes are issued in *bearer* form and *registered* form. Bearer bonds are presumed to be property of whomever has them in hand, as no record earmarks them to an individual. Lost, they're negotiable property of their finder. Registered bonds are registered to an identifiable owner.

3.   Interest may be received by presenting coupons of bearer USGs to a commercial or Federal Reserve bank or via a check in the mail. In the former case, the bond certificate comes in two portions separated by perforations: a portion representing claim to repayment of principal on the maturity date and a portion with coupons, each printed with a date of payable interest. On that date anyone with access to the bond detaches the appropriate coupon and takes it to the bank, which will give the bearer cash. Registered bonds remove threat of malappropriation. The government mails the registered owner a check every six months and a final check on maturity.

4.   Commissions for purchase of USGs vary, so shop around for a broker. They may be purchased without commission the day of initial issue. The broker or bank receives its commission from the government, not the buyer. In addition, matured USGs may be rolled over—exchanged—for new issues without cost.

5. In buying corporate bonds you have five business days to pay. USGs require immediate or next-day settlement.

SAVINGS BONDS

One of the easiest ways for investors to participate in advantages of direct ownership of USGs is through savings bonds. Savings bonds, the oldest and most maligned of American investments, are enjoying a revival, spurred by combinations of new and old profitable features. They might have a place in your portfolio if you can dismiss conventional wisdom that disparages them.

A savings bond is an obligation of the U.S. government which investors can purchase in several ways: in person at commercial banks, savings and loans, mutual savings associations, and Federal Reserve Banks; by sending a check to the Bureau of the Public Debt in Washington, D.C. 20226; or through payroll savings plans at work and with banks. (If your company has no purchase plan, you can write Department A, U.S. Savings Bonds Division, Department of the Treasury, Washington, D.C. 20226 about starting one.)

As with other USGs, the purchaser makes a loan to the federal government, and Uncle Sam is obligated to pay interest and to repay borrowed principal.

Interest paid is of two types, depending upon type of bond purchased.

The familiar EE bond is sold at discount from face value, and investors receive "accreted interest" as the difference between purchase price and face value of the bond.

The face values of EE bonds are $50, $75, $100, $200, $500, $1,000, $5,000, or $10,000. Investors pay half the face value printed on the bond. Hold the bond to maturity in 10 years from date of purchase, and you will receive face value—plus a bit more—in cash.

Series EE bonds purchased after November 1982 pay a rate of interest that increases with the age of the bond. Because of their upward-sliding interest schedule, EE bonds actually pay more than face value upon maturity: a $50 EE bond, for example, will be at least worth $52.22 at maturity.

There's another advantageous twist to this upward-sliding

interest schedule: if held for five years, EE bonds pay 85 percent of the average yield on five-year U.S. Treasury securities and are guaranteed to earn no less than guaranteed minimum interest. Whenever average yields on five-year Treasuries remain higher than the minimum interest, your $50 EE bond will mature to even more than $52.22—as, of course, will other denominations mature to more than face value.

A second type of savings bond is the HH bond, and it's like conventional corporate or municipal bonds. HH bonds are sold at face value in denominations of $500, $1,000, $5,000, and $10,000, and they mature 10 years after purchase. Instead of receiving interest as the difference between purchase price and sale price, investors receive coupon interest—in other words, a check in the mail. Investors receive twice-yearly payments until the bond matures or is cashed in.

In addition, EE and HH bonds will never be worth less than purchase price, even if cashed before maturity. Many investors bought corporate and government bonds, and when interest rates rose, market price of their bonds plummeted. That can't happen with EE or HH bonds. They're invulnerable against market loss because their prices don't vary inversely with interest rates.

However, HH bonds can be purchased and redeemed only from a Federal Reserve Bank or branch or from the Bureau of the Public Debt in Washington, D.C. 20226, or Parkersburg, West Virginia 26101. In addition, the only way to "buy" HH bonds is to exchange other savings bonds for them. More about exchange privileges in a moment.

The numerous advantages of savings bonds include more than availability in affordable denominations, federal government responsibility for principal and interest, ease of purchase (it's not much bother to exchange EE bonds for HH bonds), competitive interest rates, and immunity to market loss. Brokerage commissions aren't charged, and buying bonds doesn't require research. The government will replace them without charge if lost, stolen, or mutilated. Further, neither EE nor HH savings bonds can be called before maturity.

Three aspects of savings bonds are especially important in long-term investment programs.

First, accrued and coupon interest from savings bonds is

exempt of all but estate and federal income taxes. That can be important if you pay burdensome state, city, regional, and local taxes. The tax-exempt feature of savings bonds makes them competitive with tax-advantaged investments costing much more than $25 and $500 minimums in which savings bonds are available.

Second, although interest received from savings bonds is federally taxable, purchasers of EE bonds may declare interest income as it accrues each year, or they may postpone declaring accrued interest until the bond matures or is cashed. In other words, EE bonds are free from state and local taxes and eligible for deferral of federal taxes. That pair of tax advantages places them nearly in a class by themselves.

Third, EE bonds paying accrued interest may be exchanged for HH bonds paying coupon interest, and tax deferral continues until the HH bonds mature or are redeemed. In short, EE bonds are convertible securities, just like many preferred stocks and corporate debentures.

SAVINGS BONDS FOR CHILDREN

Let's say you're setting aside money for a child's college education. At regular intervals you can purchase EE bonds for the child. Obtain a social security number for the child. When you buy the bond, declare the child as sole owner. Each year, file a federal income tax return for the child, listing the accrued interest as yearly income.

That interest may be determined from the table in the rear of Department of the Treasury Circular, Public Debt Series, Number 1-80. It's free from a Federal Reserve Bank. Ask for Numbers 2-80 and 3-80 as well. They'll tell you everything about EE and HH bonds.

OLDER SAVINGS BONDS

Exchange of EE bonds for HH bonds works effectively whether you collect small-denomination EEs or you invest a lump sum in a large-denomination EE. The only requirements for exchanging EE for HH bonds are that the EEs must be at least six months old on the date of exchange and must have an accumulated value of $500, minimum purchase price of one HH bond.

CRITICISM OF SAVINGS BONDS

Despite their many advantages, savings bonds still suffer dismissal from "sophisticated" investors.

They're criticized for being registered and nontransferable, meaning they can't be used for collateral or resold. These aren't telling criticisms. Registered securities are safe against theft and loss because the owner is readily identifiable, and buyers of nontransferable bonds don't pay sellers interest that accumulates between semiannual payments.

Savings bonds do have impaired liquidity before six months from purchase date. If you buy a bond today and try to cash it tomorrow, the agent will tell you to return in 179 days. Whether that's a disadvantage is arguable. For spendthrifts, impaired liquidity adds discipline to an investment program. For long-term investors, temporarily impaired liquidity is no consideration because they aren't looking to turn money around within six months. In any event, after six months the bonds are liquid at any teller's cage in the country, and don't forget that the flipside advantage of impaired liquidity is stability of principal.

Some critics disparage EE bonds because they pay no current cash flow. This is a curious criticism, considering that zero coupon bonds modeled after EE bonds share this "defect" yet they're the most popular novelty on Wall Street. In addition, many applauded investments pay no current yield, including dividendless stocks, precious metals, land, and collectibles.

Another point often made against savings bonds is that they pay less interest than competing investments. That may hold true for larger sums, but we have to distinguish between investing accumulated capital and accumulating investment capital.

The megabuck investor who's accumulated a wad of capital can receive higher interest or dividend returns than savings bonds pay. Among other choices, the well-heeled could, in fact, buy a five-year Treasury bond and receive its full rate of interest instead of buying EE bonds and receiving 85 percent of the five-year bond rate paid by EEs—assuming they also wish to pay commissions, pay accrued interest to the seller, pay yearly federal tax on coupon interest, and risk capital loss if interest rates increase.

On the other hand, if you're accumulating investment capital, remember that EE bonds pay governmentally guaranteed, tax-deferred, tax-exempt interest on amounts as small as $25. You can't buy part of a five-year Treasury bond for $25, but with $25 you can buy a whole EE bond yielding close to what you'd earn if you'd bought the other Treasury security outright.

But lest you think that savings bonds are strictly for poorhouse investors, consider the assessment of Benjamin Graham, in *The Intelligent Investor:*[1] "U.S. savings bonds still possess certain unique merits that make them a suitable purchase by any individual investor."

AGENCY PAPER

Many governmental agencies issue bonds, and often their yields are higher. Some *agency paper* is also guaranteed by the Treasury. Public Housing Authority Bonds, issued by local officials to finance low-income dwellings, are backed by the Federal Housing Assistance Administration, which means they're backed by the same full faith and credit as outright USGs. Other agency paper, although not strictly guaranteed by the Treasury, is issued by congressionally authorized organizations, so it's generally supposed Uncle Sam wouldn't allow default. Still other paper, like that of the World Bank, has no direct affiliation with the U.S. government, but conventional wisdom holds that the Treasury would intervene against default.

The yields, maturities, guarantees, uses, prices, and special considerations of agency paper are so diverse as to require their own book to explain. For instance, agency yields quoted in the financial press are yields to maturity, not current yield. Bonds issued by the Government National Mortgage Association ("Ginnie Mae") pay monthly interest, unlike semiannual

---

[1]New York: Harper & Row, 1973

interest with conventional USGs, but it is varying interest—you don't get a check for the same amount every month (the reason is that GNMAs are pools of individual mortgages of varying maturities and interest payments, some of which mature to be replaced by higher-interest mortgages, some of which don't and aren't, and none of which is identical).

There is one other consideration that prohibits our extended discussion of these securities: price. Minimum purchase amounts to buy these securities range from $25,000 to $1 million and more. Whereas small investors can buy USGs for $1,000 to $5,000, they're priced out of agencies. They're not, however, excluded from indirect ownership, because for $1,000 to $5,000, investors can participate in pools of agency securities assembled in the mode of mutual funds or unit trusts.

Mutual funds rate their own chapter, so we'll not go into them now. In addition, money market funds, a type of mutual fund also featured in its own chapter, offer investors the chance to put cash into agencies, sometimes in constant-dollar investments that avoid price fluctuations. Unit trusts, however, appear forthwith, and they're excellent for small investors wanting to purchase agency securities indirectly.

UNIT TRUST

A *unit trust* is an unmanaged collection of agency bonds made available to investors in amounts less than outright purchase of the included securities. Unit trusts are usually sponsored by brokerages and advertised in the financial and general circulation press. Their name derives from individual investor's purchasing portions (units) of a larger portfolio. In contrast to a mutual fund bond portfolio, to which fund managers add and delete securities, a unit trust includes specific securities which are rarely changed.

When a brokerage house brings a unit trust to market, a fixed number of shares is offered for sale. When that number is sold, subscription is closed. Those who invest in the trust receive a prorated share of the total return from pooled securities. In general, one unit of the trust will be priced from $1,000 to $1,050, with a minimum investment being five units; however, some brokerages allow purchase of single units. Typically, the return for each investor is identical to the return obtained by the total portfolio because unit trusts are *pass-through* securities. The term means that returns from the portfolio are distributed directly to its constituent owners. The brokerage assembling the unit trust receives compensation from sales charges, not from returns on investment.

As securities in the trust mature, investors' capital is returned along with interest brought by the investments. Accordingly, payments often include return of principal as well as interest. That's especially true of unit trusts investing in mortgage-backed securities, such as the Ginnie Maes mentioned a moment ago.

Returns are usually mailed to the trust's owners monthly, although some trusts arrange for reinvestment in the original trust or in another. Also, some brokerages will establish interest-bearing accounts, usually money market funds, into which trust income is placed to earn additional interest. These arrangements permit additional compounding of returns.

Unit trusts have varying maturities, depending upon types of securities in the trust, with 5 to 12 years being standard. Although government agency paper is a common unit trust investment, some trusts invest in six-month certificates of deposit, varying maturities of USGs, corporate and municipal bonds, and even stocks, usually high-yielding utility stocks. When the total maturity of the trust is reached, the brokerage closes it—and usually invites investors to participate in a new trust.

Often the brokerage assembling the trust will maintain a secondary market through which investors can buy and sell their holdings. As always, sellers cashing in before maturity may receive more or less than the amount initially invested.

Trusts frequently offer attractive yields. As of 1987, for example, unit trusts of Government National Mortgage Association paper yield around 9 percent, compared with 7 to 8 percent for USGs and 6 percent for T-bills. Other advantages are diversification and ability to invest in a portfolio of investments that otherwise would be priced beyond reach.

The chief disadvantage of trusts is the sales charge, often 5 to 8 percent of invested capital, although they are occasionally available without charge. Nonetheless, it may be a small price compared with the otherwise inaccessible cost of direct investment in securities included within the unit trust. If units are selling at a premium, the amount of the premium may not be claimed as a capital loss.

STATE AND LOCAL BONDS

States, cities, municipalities, and revenue districts also sell bonds. The chief appeal of *municipal bonds* or munies is that most of them pay interest exempt from federal taxation. Also, some states and cities exempt interest on their own municipals from state taxation. Municipals offering coincidence of untaxed income are called double dippers.

As a consequence of their privileged tax status, munies usually provide a smaller absolute yield than fully taxed securities. Just to pick figures by way of illustration, munies may be offering 5 to 8 percent coupon yields when fully taxed bonds of similar quality are paying 10 percent.

Accordingly, munies are often evaluated according to *taxable equivalent yields*—comparison of aftertax yield on one investment with the untaxed yield of munies.

There's a quick way to calculate whether you're better off with municipals or other securities by computing taxable equivalent yields. Look up your anticipated income and tax bracket in the tax booklets the IRS mails yearly. Examine the yield from the municipal bond. Finally, plug those figures into the formula $TF = BT(1 - t)$.

TF is the tax-free return from munies. BT is the before-tax return available from other investments. The t is your marginal tax rate from the IRS booklet.

Let's say the tax-free yield on the municipal bond is 9 percent. The before-tax yield on other investments is 12 percent. Your tax bracket is 14 percent. Then:

$$TF = .12 \ (1-.14)$$
$$TF = .12 \ (.86)$$
$$TF = .1032 \text{ or } 10.32 \text{ percent}$$

These calculations show the equivalent yield of the taxable investment is 10.32 percent. That means if you put your money into the fully taxed investment yielding 10 percent and pay your taxes, you're better off than by putting your money into the municipal bond paying 9 percent without taxation.

MUNIES PRO AND CON

For small investors, the problem with direct ownership of munies is twofold: (1) the tax-exempt feature is so compelling that investors may ignore higher posttax returns from other investments; (2) munies are generally sold in minimum denominations of $5,000.

There are many types of munies, but generally they fall into the category of *general obligations* (GOBs) or *revenue bonds*. Both come in varying maturities, and shorter maturities are generally called notes, as distinguished from longer-maturing bonds.

The difference between GOBs and revenue bonds is their backing. General obligation bonds or notes are backed by the full faith and credit of the borrowing municipality. As the term implies, these are general obligations, and interest plus principal are met from general revenues of the issuer. That means tax revenues, as a practical matter.

Revenue bonds are issued by water project authorities, sewer districts, highway commissions, and public works activities to construct specific projects. Interest and principal are paid from revenues of the project for which bonds were issued. If the project doesn't produce sufficient revenues, bondholders don't receive their money. Tax authorities are not obligated to guarantee interest and principal. However, some revenue bonds *are* backed by specific taxes, commonly gasoline taxes.

Straight revenue bonds are riskier than general obligation bonds, but sometimes risk is reduced by intervention of guarantors. In some instances a state or community will obligate itself to guarantee a revenue bond, in which case it approaches the security of a GOB and is called a double-barreled bond because of dual backing by project revenues and general revenues. In addition, some revenue bonds are guaranteed by major corporations. These issues are most commonly called *industrial development revenue bonds* (IDRs) or *pollution control revenue bonds* (PCBs), both named by the purpose they support.

For example, a corporation and a community agree their

mutual benefit can be served by the corporation's building a plant nearby. However, current corporate-level interest rates may prohibit the corporation from floating bonds to finance the plant. In such case, the corporation loses the chance for expansion and the community loses jobs the corporation would have created and enlarged revenues from corporate, sales, and personal taxes.

Therefore, the community may lend its name to the raising of money for construction of the corporate facility. The corporation floats a Loose Gravel, Nebraska, Industrial Development Revenue Bond, Series A, for which it pays lower municipal bond interest rates instead of higher corporate bond rates. The corporation guarantees interest and principal, not the community. As a consequence, the corporation gets its plant, the city gets jobs and tax revenues, and investors get tax-exempt municipal bond interest.

These financing arrangements serve many directly and indirectly beneficial purposes to corporations, communities, and citizens. It is unfortunate that post-1986 tax laws curtail sharply new issues of IDRs and PCBs.

The federal government acts as guarantor for some munies, usually those issued by public housing authorities. This convenient arrangement offers the best of all investment worlds—tax-free income guaranteed by the federal government.

As we noted, munies are generally offered in $5,000 denominations and are purchased and sold through stockbrokers. Although individual bonds may be in $1,000 denominations, purchase of five is usually the minimum permitted lot. Anything other than a five-bond group is difficult to resell, so an investor contemplating munies faces a $5,000 outlay. When initially offered to the public, munies may be purchased without commission. Thereafter, commissions apply to purchase and sale.

Munies are generally considered very safe, commonly ranking next to USGs and agencies, and municipal bond defaults are rare. But life has been tough for states and municipalities. In response to uncertainties now associated with municipal governments, some companies offer insurance for municipal bonds. Generally, insurance is paid by the issuer, but it may be possible for individual owners of munies to have portfolios insured against default. The stockbroker from whom you purchase munies should have information about insurance.

Municipal bonds resemble corporate bonds, except it's more common to find munies in bearer form. Arrangements can be made to have bearer munies registered to you for a fee. Otherwise, they can be left in custody of a stockbroker. Interest is paid twice yearly, commonly the first day of the appropriate month. A variety of maturity dates is common, ranging from 1 to 20 years or more. Like corporates, the market price of munies varies inversely to interest rates.

As a consequence of increased awareness of munies, financial institutions have burned the midnight oil to find ways investors can receive tax-advantaged income through indirect ownership of munies. Among the most convenient means of indirect ownership of munies is through mutual funds specializing in municipal securities. These are discussed in the next chapter. More recently, money market funds offer tax-exempt income, discussed in Chapter Nine.

Like USGs and agencies, municipals are available through unit trusts called *municipal investment trusts*. In general, unit trusts also require $5,000 investments, although $1,000 minimums are becoming common. Municipal unit trusts offer monthly returns as opposed to semiannual returns provided by direct ownership of munies. Municipal unit trusts are offered through brokerages and are frequently advertised.

Finally, even munies have caught the zero coupon craze. Some are issued originally as zeros, with the difference between purchase price and maturity value (sometimes called compound accreted value) being tax-free interest. They can be useful for investors wishing long-term, federally tax-free income. Consult Donald Nichols, *The Dow Jones-Irwin Guide to Zero Coupon Investments*,[2] for complete discussion of municipal zeros.

SUMMARY

It's time to sum up possibilities offered small investors through direct ownership of U.S Treasury, agency, and municipal securities.

---

[2]Homewood, Ill.: Dow Jones-Irwin, 1986.

Available in minimums of $25 to $5,000, USGs offer safe, liquid investment with a range of maturities. Interest is paid twice yearly (except for EE bonds) by check or coupon and is exempt from state income tax. Although commissions normally apply to purchase and sale of USGs (savings bonds excepted), they may be obtained without fee when initially issued or by rolling over matured bonds. Series EE savings bonds offer tax-deferred interest and conversion to HH bonds.

The chief disadvantage to direct ownership of USGs (other than savings bonds) is that they are available in minimum units of $1,000 to $5,000. This disadvantage is overcome by indirect ownership via mutual and money market funds.

Agency securities offer similar advantages plus higher interest, except that minimum purchase amounts are too high for the investor with only $5,000 to spend. To overcome this difficulty, investors may own them indirectly through unit trusts for investments of $1,000 to $5,000. Unit trusts offer the further advantage of monthly income.

Municipal bonds and notes offer investors income exempt from federal income tax and in some cases exempt from state income tax. They are generally safe, and guarantors add to their safety. For the most part, investors must be prepared to buy munies in $5,000 minimums.

Municipal securities are also offered through unit trusts and other vehicles of indirect ownership. Zero coupon munies are available either as initial issues of new bonds or from financial intermediaries that have assembled packages of municipal bonds and marketed them as zeros.

As is true of any fixed-income security, government bonds are subject to price fluctuations that may result in capital losses if the investor must sell at inopportune times (again, EE and HH bonds excepted, for they may always be redeemed for at least purchase price). Also, fixed-income investors must be conscious of effects of inflation on the unchanging income stream. These drawbacks considered, government bonds can be important—and perhaps essential—components of the small investor's portfolio.

Indirect Ownership of Corporate and Government Securities: Investment Companies

For reasons reviewed by chapters on direct ownership of stocks and bonds, small investors seeking to construct a portfolio are in for a time of it.

First, there was the problem of market timing. Securities markets have doldrums like anyone else, and sometimes you have to leave them alone to work out their distress. Then there was the problem of picking securities. At any cycle of the market, someone will be holding the losers, and the likelihood is it will be the novice investor.

Diversification was another problem. Investors with only $5,000 likely won't achieve a diversified portfolio. Cost was a further consideration. Many securities, both stocks and bonds, are too expensive for investors of modest means to own directly. And there were commissions and the odd lot differential, which devour investment capital.

MUTUAL FUNDS

The simplest way to avoid these dilemmas is through indirect ownership of securities: buying shares of companies that buy shares of other companies. That circular definition describes *open-end investment companies*, better known as *mutual funds*.

Here's a description from Steuart B. Mead in *Mutual Funds*:[1]

> A mutual fund is a pool of investors' money, brought together by fund managers and invested by them, on behalf of the investors, in a widely diversified list of corporate stocks, corporate bonds, and government bonds. Each investor in a mutual fund is a shareholder of the mutual fund. All gains and losses of the fund are prorated to each share. It is an indirect method of security ownership.

That's what mutual funds do. They are investment companies that assemble money from many people and buy stocks and bonds on their behalf. All these people own shares in the investment company, and the assets of the company are securities rather than plant and equipment. As a subscriber to a mutual fund, you own stock in a company whose business is buying stocks—or, to phrase the matter awkwardly and somewhat imprecisely if you subscribe to a bond fund, you own stock in bonds. This company is run—that is, investments are made—by professional money managers who have access to securities exchanges and to legions of data. If the investment company picks securities that increase in price, shares of the mutual fund increase in price.

The price of mutual fund shares is called net asset value, or NAV. It is the price per share of a mutual fund and is equivalent to the share price of a stock or the purchase price of a bond. Net asset value is calculated by dividing the value of the fund's total portfolio by the number of shares outstanding. When securities purchased by mutual funds increase in price, the net asset value of the fund's shares increases. Conversely, if securities held by your fund decrease in price, your fund's net asset value decreases. Your fund performs as the securities it holds perform, and the measure of performance is increase or decrease in NAV.

One attractive aspect of net asset value is that it allows investors to purchase fractional shares. That's not the case with direct ownership of stock or bonds. If you have $1,000 and want

---

[1]Braintree, Mass.: D. H. Mark Publishing, 1971.

to buy AT&T stock at, say, $21 per share, you can buy 47 shares. If you send your $1,000 to a mutual fund with a net asset value of $21, you'll buy 47.619 shares (funds usually carry fractional shares to three decimals).

Most mutual funds are offered by investment groups through an arrangement commonly called a family of funds. Each fund contains many securities, and each investment group offers many funds, each with differing goals. Just to pick one family— the highly imitated Fidelity Investment Group—and one type of investment—corporate stocks—consider the following individual mutual funds to choose from:

The Fidelity Trend Fund hopes to make money by buying stocks that lead the market upward or maintain their prices as the general market falls. In contrast, Fidelity ContraFund purchases stocks "out of favor" with investors, who presumably will recognize their mistake and rush, money in hand, to correct it. Magellan Fund, gunslinger of the Fidelity family, invests for aggressive capital gains. The Fidelity Equity-Income Fund strives to balance capital gains and income from dividends. The Puritan Fund concentrates on income.

Each mutual fund within the Fidelity Investment Group tries to be a winner with philosophies that often contradict each other. Consider ContraFund and Trend.

ContraFund is looking for the Liza Doolittle it can make into a lady. On the other hand, Trend fancies itself as Big Man on Campus, the kind of fund who rides with the homecoming queen every year. Presumably Trend wouldn't cast a second look at a stock ContraFund brought home to meet its investment committee. But when the stock shows up in the market wearing its first strapless gown and all the other funds are asking "Where have you been all my life?" Trend is likely to pick up a few shares with its I-can-make-you-a-star routine. Yet the moment Trend decides the little sylph is a hot number is the moment ContraFund thinks it's too popular.

Both Trend and ContraFund can be wrong, but both can't be right—at least not about the same stock at the same time. However, there are many stocks in the market, and there are many courtship rituals under way, and both funds will find stocks to love and be loved by.

Fidelity Investment Group is one of scores of fund families.

Literally hundreds of investment houses have mutual funds. If one fund in the family doesn't treat you so well, you can date its sister. They all have the same phone number. In addition, most major brokerage firms offer mutual funds.

INVESTMENT IN STOCK FUNDS

Let's look in more detail at investment possibilities of mutual funds. We'll talk about two general types: funds that invest largely in stocks, and funds that invest largely in bonds.

The importance of stock funds, apart from advantages of diversification and professional management, is that investors can find funds that suit the objectives for which they've decided to invest in stocks. You'll recall from Chapter Five that three objectives from stock ownership are aggressive capital gains, long-term capital gains, and income. The elegance of mutual funds is that they meet investors' desires in reaching each of these goals.

Investors seeking aggressive gains may choose funds which strive to meet that goal through purchase of securities promising fast capital growth. Some aggressive funds are so committed to their goal that they will *sell short* (sell securities in hopes their prices will fall and repurchase at the lower price), purchase securities on margin (borrow money from brokers to buy stocks), and even borrow money from banks with which to purchase securities margined with brokers. With some aggressive growth funds, anything legal goes. Other funds, though still aggressive, aren't so vigorous in pursuit of a kill.

Similarly, investors seeking measured capital growth can find hundreds of funds catering to their objectives. The revelry of soaring prices doesn't suit the temperament of long-term investors, and they can find a fund that suits their preferences, just as aggressive investors may subscribe to a fund matching theirs.

Income investors likewise may subscribe to mutual funds concentrating their efforts on high-dividend stocks. Some funds, for example, invest exclusively in stocks of public utilities, long noted for attractive dividend payments. Other income funds may seek dividend-paying stocks temporarily suppressed in price, making yields attractive, while awaiting the market to revalue prices upward. A few income funds hold preferred stocks because dividend payments are often more attractive than common stocks. Also, as mentioned, some funds strive for balance of capital gains and income.

Generally, stock funds will concentrate their portfolios on common stocks. However, stock funds often spread holdings to include preferreds and bonds for several reasons. At a given stage of the market, bonds may be paying substantial interest. The manager of an income fund may decide to increase holdings of bonds in order to meet the fund's income objectives. Also, the manager of a growth fund may have positions in convertible preferreds and convertible bonds, claiming income from dividends and interest while hoping to exercise the convertible if the underlying stock increases in price.

Mutual funds are astonishingly diverse in objectives, market viewpoints, and clientele. There are funds that invest only in emerging companies or only in mature corporations. There are funds that invest only in medical companies or high-tech companies or mining companies or insurance companies. The Oceanographic Fund buys shares in companies doing aquatic business. There are funds that refuse to buy stocks of tobacco, alcohol, munitions, and chemical corporations. There are mutual funds that invest from the rigid belief the world economy will disintegrate at any moment. They are contested by funds that believe the financial best is yet to come. There's a fund that invests only in companies operating in Kansas or Missouri, and, not to be outdone in its specificity, there's another fund that invests in corporations operating in Rochester, New York. There are mutual funds exclusively for doctors, dentists, teachers, and probably—one wouldn't be surprised—Indian chiefs. Some mutual funds invest in shares of other mutual funds. Name an industry, an opinion about the economy, or a population group, and there will be a mutual fund serving it.

Managers of mutual funds pour over the thousands of reports and data available to them, and depending upon objectives of the fund—income, short-term gains, long-term gains— pick stocks likely in their view to achieve their goals. In turn, many publications review the intentions and performance of mutual funds and report on them. One such publication is the *Growth Fund Guide*, "a service that tells you what it thinks and why.''[2] Another is the *No-load Mutual Fund Guide* by William E. Donoghue with Thomas Tilling.[3]

INVESTMENT IN CORPORATE BOND FUNDS

Mutual funds investing in stocks aren't the only types available. Although many equity funds purchase corporate bonds for their portfolios, some funds specialize in exclusive purchases of corporate obligations. Corporate bond funds usually try to achieve a high current return consistent with preservation of capital, although many bond funds have more specific goals.

Some, for example, purchase lower-rated bonds for maximum current income. Others invest strictly in blue-chip bonds or in those rated above a certain level. Still other funds buy bonds selling at deep discounts and go after capital appreciation, either holding the bonds until they mature or selling them if their prices rise. In short, mutual funds offer bonds in a range of objectives, just as they offer stocks.

As always, picking a bond fund depends upon your objectives. If you're willing to accept market risk in exchange for the chance of higher returns, you might want to consider aggressive bond funds. Or perhaps you're playing it conservative with bonds as a backup to a swinging stock fund. Or the other way around. As with choosing an equities fund, *consider* what you really want when investigating a mutual fund of bonds.

Apart from differing in their investment goals, bond funds are of two types: those which have no set maturity and those which do.

The former is more common, because one defining characteristic of open-end investment companies is that they continually offer and redeem shares, alter composition of bonds in their portfolios, and intend to remain in business indefinitely. Funds with no maturity attempt to provide market-level returns continually.

---

[2]This guide is available from Growth Fund Research, Inc., Growth Fund Research Building M-8, Yreka, California 96097.

[3]New York: Harper & Row, 1983.

However, many mutual fund families also offer bond funds with fixed maturities—sometimes called *target funds*. These funds operate for a set period, usually 5 to 15 years, after which they fold up their portfolio and disburse assets to the fund's owners. Sometimes target funds are offered to the public for a restricted period, and sometimes you can purchase shares in target funds up to the day before final maturity. Unless market conditions or creditworthiness of issuers deteriorates, target funds will generally not be active traders. In some cases, target funds will purchase bonds maturing on the date of the fund's total maturity and merely hold the securities. Target funds attempt to provide a set, predictable rate of income and capital appreciation.

The chief advantage to maturity-free bond funds is that you can always enter and withdraw at any time. You may also make subsequent investments in the fund at your convenience.

Prices of maturity-free funds fluctuate with general bond market conditions. This is an advantage and a disadvantage. When interest rates are high and bond prices suppressed, you can enter a bond fund and wait for rates to fall and prices to rise, realizing capital gains along with interest income. On the other hand, if you aren't adept at following interest rates, you may find yourself doing the opposite: riding bond prices down as interest rates rise. In short, conventional bond funds don't offer price stability and a predictable rate of return.

Target funds, as a generality, deliver a predictable rate of return. In addition, some target funds are legally arranged to capture tax advantages of annuities, discussed in Chapter Eleven.

If the target fund is available to the public for only a brief period, you may not be able to buy into the fund at your convenience. Also, in some cases, subsequent investment is prohibited. Further, when the target fund matures, you have the problem of reinvesting your income, meaning you may wind up back in a conventional bond fund anyway.

Some target funds may have impaired liquidity, meaning you might not be able to get your money if you need it unexpectedly. Then again, because bond prices will fluctuate, you may not receive the full amount of your initial investment if you can and do sell out your fund before maturity. Obviously, you must check special features of a target fund carefully.

INVESTMENT IN GOVERNMENT BOND FUNDS

So far we've been concerned with bond funds which invest in corporate obligations. However, many fund families offer funds that invest in government and municipal bonds. These, too, are worth consideration.

Virtually every fund family offers a bond fund which invests exclusively in obligations of the U.S. government and its agencies. Some of these funds fluctuate in price; that is, the NAV of their shares rises and falls with market conditions. Others, to be discussed in the chapter on money market funds, maintain a constant NAV.

These government bond funds purchase Treasury bills, notes, and bonds, securities of federal agencies such as the Government National Mortgage Association, and—less frequently—issues from nongovernmental agencies that are backed by a pledge of repayment from the government. Some shipping and transportation companies, for example, issue bonds backed by a governmental pledge to bail holders out if the company gets into financial trouble.

The chief advantage of government bond funds is security. The bonds they purchase are backed by the full faith and credit of the United States. Unless the U.S. government goes under— in which case we'd have more to worry about than money—you will receive payments of principal and interest. Default risk is virtually nonexistent. Typically, however, government bond funds pay slightly less interest than corporate bond funds because of their safety.

A special note: depending upon the fund to which you subscribe, returns received from a government bond fund may be classified as dividends and not interest because of the way the IRS has interpreted things. This means you pay state and local tax on income from government bond *funds* even though you would be exempt from such taxation if you owned the bonds directly.

Virtually every mutual fund family offers a fund which

deals in securities issued by states, cities, counties, municipalities, districts, and revenue project authorities. As with federal government bond funds, many *municipal bond funds* have a constant-dollar share price. However, again we defer discussion of those until the chapter on money market funds. For now, we will be aware that municipal bond funds fluctuate in price as do all the other mutual funds.

The chief advantage of municipal bond funds is that their interest payments are exempt from federal income tax. Their appeal is to investors in higher tax brackets. Because of their tax advantages, municipal bonds and municipal bond funds pay less interest than their taxable counterparts.

However, the tax status of municipal bond funds is a bit more complicated than it appears.

Capital gains the municipal bond fund accrues are fully taxable. At the end of the year your account statement will reveal the portion of capital gains distributed to you.

Second, many states do not tax interest payments on their own securities in general, or else selected municipal issues will be exempt from state taxation. We discussed "double dippers" in Chapter Seven. If your municipal bond fund holds these securities, you need not pay state taxes on that portion of interest. Often municipal bond funds publish a distribution of income statement. If, for example, 6 percent of the fund's total interest income was received from securities issued by your state, and if your state does not tax those securities, you may subtract 6 percent of your fund income from state taxation.

All things considered, it's probably easier just to forget about calculating how much income from municipal bond funds you can exclude from the governor. To be absolutely certain, you'd have to consult a tax specialist. Perhaps your state isn't one that exempts its own bonds from taxation. And any possible tax advantages likely won't be worth the effort of digging.

Two notes of warning about municipal bond funds bear repeating from Chapter Seven:

First, tax advantages of municipal bond funds are greater as your tax bracket increases. If you're in a relatively low tax bracket, or if you have deductions that decrease your tax liability substantially, you often can receive more from investment in fully taxable funds.

The second warning about municipal bonds is their security. Security of your investment depends upon ability of the state, city, or tax district to meet its payments. That ability may not be immediately suspect, but circumstances can change. Witness misfortunes of New York City and Cleveland and the Washington State Public Power Authority.

Perhaps in recognition of these concerns, most mutual fund families offer more than one municipal bond fund, each with a stated intention of buying municipal bonds with a given "rating." Major rating agencies—Moody's, Standard & Poor's, and others—rate municipal bonds in addition to corporate securities according to safety of principal and interest. The higher the rating, the lower the interest paid by the issuer and received by the owner. Some mutual funds state they buy securities "rated AAA" or "rated A or better," with AAA, AA, A, and BBB being investment grade municipal bonds. Other funds purchase lower-rated bonds with the intention of pursuing higher yields for accepting greater risk.

THE PROSPECTUS

Once you've decided a particular mutual fund will serve your investment objectives—be it one of the many types of stock or bond funds—you're ready to invest. Once you have an inkling that a particular fund might suit your purposes, call or write for the prospectus. It's a document which the fund must provide prospective (hence the name) investors. The prospectus must list such important information as the fund's goals, restrictions, advisers, fees, and portfolio.

Entire books have been written on how to read a prospectus. Investors contemplating large deposits in a mutual fund would be wise to become familiar with the jargon and intricacies the prospectus contains. For most investors, familiarity with basics will suffice for intelligent decisions.

In reading the prospectus, be aware of the kinds of stocks and bonds the fund holds. If the fund promotes itself as a conservative vehicle and the prospectus shows holdings of high-flying stocks and lower-rated bonds, the fund isn't being consistent.

Next, examine minimums for initial and subsequent investments. Some funds require an initial investment of up to $10,000, with subsequent investments being $1,000 or more. Other funds have no minimums. As an average, stock funds will have initial investment requirements of $1,000 to $2,500 with subsequent investment purchases being $50 to $500. If the initial investment is more than you can afford, or if subscribing to a fund will tilt your investment program away from other investments, consider a cheaper fund.

Look also at the fund's fees and charges. Most mutual funds are *load* or *no-load* funds. Funds that charge a load, also called *front-end load*, will deduct a percentage of your investment before investing your money. Load range from 1 to 8 percent of initial investment and represent a substantial deduction from invested capital. For example, if you send $1,000 to a fund with an 8 percent load, the fund keeps $80 for fees and invests $920 for you. If the minimum subsequent investment is $250 and the fund charges a 2 percent load on subsequent investments, you have only $245 working for you. With that much taken off the top, a fund would have to have substantial performance just for you to break even.

By the way, some mutual funds are available only through stockbrokers, who charge commissions for mailing application forms you filled out, and some funds charge closeout or transfer fees that may be 1 or 2 percent of the account balance.

Once you've examined investment minimums and fees, look to see how often the fund sends statements of account and how often earnings from the fund are distributed to your account. Most funds mail quarterly statements and confirmation statements each time you make a subsequent deposit in the fund.

Distribution of interest, dividends, and capital gains to your account is a different and more irregular matter. Funds distribute earnings from their portfolio regularly, although "regularly" may mean every quarter in the case of income funds or once a year in the case of aggressive growth funds.

Finally, examine the fund's record. Ideally, you want a fund that's performed well in up and down markets. The past is no proof of the future, but it's the only hint you have. The prospectus will usually give a thumbnail review of performance during the past few years. If that information is absent, there are several ways to hunt up past performance.

You can dial the toll-free number in the prospectus and ask the fund's service representative how the fund has fared—or you may inquire about any of the considerations we've raised. Most personal investment magazines in general circulation—*Money* is worthwhile—will have devoted an issue to mutual fund performance. Go the the library for current and previous issues. While you're there, ask if the library carries *Lipper's Analytical Service*, an exhaustive guide to mutual fund comparisons. If the Library doesn't have a copy, check a local college business library.

As long as we're on this subject of information, it's worth mentioning that once you request materials from a fund you'll be placed on a mailing list. Free mailings can be useful. Also, you might take an investment course offered by an adult education program. As a student, subscribe to *The Wall Street Journal* at student rates. In addition, the local office of a brokerage firm often holds seminars for potential clients. You can attend without obligation.

THE APPLICATION

Occasionally an application will require your signature to be verified by a broker, banker, or savings and loan officer. A notary can't fill this requirement. More frequently, funds constituted as partnerships and funds that offer checking privileges will insist upon signature verification. But in nearly all cases your John Hancock on the dotted line will be sufficient to enroll you.

While completing the application, mark appropriate spaces for special services you want. For instance, the fund may ask if you want telephone withdrawal or transfer privileges that allow you to conduct business over the phone. There may be a special bloc to request checking privileges.

You must specify if you wish earnings from the fund reinvested in additional shares or mailed directly to you. Mutual funds offer the chance for dividends, interest, and capital gains to be reinvested in additional shares of the fund, or you may elect distributions paid by check. You may also elect an intermediate choice: have capital gains reinvested in additional shares and dividends paid by check, or vice versa.

If your account is large, you may have automatic withdrawals made to you from the fund. Like receiving distributions in cash, receiving automatic withdrawals can be useful for investors who need current income. Conversely, if you're building a mutual fund investment, you may have automatic investments taken from a checking or savings account and deposited in your fund.

Most funds ask if you wish to possess certificates as evidence of ownership. These certificates resemble stock certificates, and there's no reason you should want this confirmation of ownership. For one thing, regular communications from the fund will detail your holdings. For another, if you withdraw from the fund you'll have to complete the certificates and mail them back, entailing unnecessary delays and paperwork.

YOU AS SHAREHOLDER

After completing the application, you mail a check or money order to the fund, and you're a shareholder. Bank wire transfers may also be used for enrolling, but a fee is charged by the wiring bank. In most cases you can open an account over the phone with a promise that your initial deposit and completed application are forthcoming.

In a few weeks you'll receive confirmation from the fund, and you'll also receive a stub for use in subsequent purchases of shares. There are several important entries to examine when you receive confirmation of subscription.

First, make sure your name and names of co-owners are spelled correctly and that social security numbers are accurate. Check that the identification number on the confirmation matches the stub used for subsequent investments. If there's a difference, subsequent investments may be credited to someone else's account.

Next, notice the net asset value of the fund's shares on the day you subscribed. This is the price of the shares that you paid to enter the fund, and it is the base upon which you'll evaluate the fund's performance while you're a shareholder.

The amount you initially invested, minus any load, divided by net asset value will be the number of shares you own. Thereafter, you need merely multiply the number of shares you own times stated NAV printed in the mutual fund section in the financial pages to keep track of performance.

When you make subsequent investments you will receive a purchase confirmation, and your fund will send you regular records of amounts reinvested. Don't confuse subsequent investment with reinvestment. The former is your active decision to purchase additional shares in the fund by check or money order; the latter is the fun's reinvesting your earnings in additional shares for your account. Records of subsequent investment and reinvestment reveal the amounts invested, the NAV at which shares were purchased, the number of newly acquired shares, and the total number of shares acquired along with dates of all transactions.

When you wish to withdraw from a fund, you can sell shares—*redeem* is the term—by calling the fund if you've so specified in your initial account application. Otherwise, you'll have to send written notice of your intention to withdraw. On the day you leave the fund, someone will calculate the number of shares you own, multiply it by the fund's net asset value, subtract any closing fees, and mail you a check for the remainder. You need not sell all of your shares. Most funds will allow you to sell part of your holdings, subject to minimum withdrawals and account balances.

FUND TAX STATUS

Now that all dividends and capital gains are taxed as ordinary income, tax status of mutual funds is less complicated. Many funds pay all returns as *dividends*, even though substantial portions of their returns are capital gains. Some mutual fund dividend payments *are* outright dividends as strictly defined; that is, they represent payments by corporations to owners of their stock. However, some funds report distributions as capital gains and/or dividends, both to you and to the IRS. You must

account for receipt of dividends and capital gains in the appropriate sections of your federal 1040. At the end of each year,
your fund will mail you Form 1099 detailing type of distributions you've received.

FUNDS' VERSATILITY

Mutual funds are incredibly versatile, and no discussion would
be complete without mentioning your ability to manage a portfolio of indirectly held securities.

By subscribing to a fund family you have exchange privileges with other funds in the family. As your investment goals
change you can move from one type of investment to another by
exchanging shares of one fund for shares of another fund within
the family. You can restructure an entire portfolio with a
call. You give instructions to the fund's representatives, and
you've got a new set of stocks or bonds.

It's difficult to overstate advantages investors enjoy through
exchange privileges. You can move with market conditions.
Say you expect economic conditions to be rocky, with negative
results for stocks in general. A call moves your money into
another type of investment—say, a money fund or a government bond fund. On the other hand, if you think circumstances
favor stocks, you can do the converse—move out of bonds and
into funds investing in stocks. You can be even more specific
within categories of investments. Perhaps you want to move
out of a stock fund concentrating on income and into a stock
fund pursuing vigorous capital gains. You can do so with a call.

CLOSED-END FUNDS

Although mutual funds are the most readily available means of
indirectly owning securities, they are not the only means. Remember that "mutual fund" is the colloquial name for an open-
end investment company. There is another type of fund known
as a *closed-end investment company.*

Like mutual funds, closed-end investment companies pool
money for purchase of securities. Unlike mutual funds, closed-
end funds issue a fixed number of shares. They neither issue
new shares nor redeem old shares. Shares of closed-ends are

purchased through a broker, and they are listed on the major exchanges like other stocks. If you wish to cash in your closed-end shares, you do not redeem them through the fund. Instead, you must call your broker and sell them as you would any directly held stock.

Like mutual funds, closed-ends compute their net asset value by dividing portfolio value by number of shares outstanding. However, because closed-ends are sold through stock exchanges, market conditions establish their selling price, not net asset value. Accordingly, closed-end shares often sell at a discount or premium—that is, less than or more than net asset value.

Many observers suggest that closed-ends selling at a discount to NAV promise built-in capital gains, the assumption being that eventually these shares must sell at what they're "intrinsically worth." The argument seems reasonable, but not realistic. Once shares sell below net asset value, there's no reason why the discount shouldn't persist or even deepen. Nonetheless, closed-ends selling at discounts may eventually attain full NAV.

Every Monday *The Wall Street Journal* publishes a list of closed-end funds, including their net asset values, selling prices, and the difference between the two. The most ready source of information about closed-ends is a stockbroker. Generally, closed-ends are similar to open-end funds in investment policies, restrictions, and goals. Like some mutual funds, some closed-ends are highly specialized in a particular industry or type of investment.

DUAL FUNDS

There are many subcategories of closed-end investment companies, and one of interest to the small investor is the *dual fund*. Dual funds have two classes of shares: income and capital. The idea behind this division is that some investors are interested solely in income and others solely in capital gains. The dual fund brings these two types of investors together in a portfolio to multiply advantages to both.

Although dual funds are purchased through brokers and listed on major exchanges like other closed-end investment companies, they have an expiration date, unlike either mutual funds or other closed-ends. In that respect they are akin to target funds offered by bond mutual funds.

Throughout the life of the fund, income investors receive all dividends or interest paid by stocks or bonds in the portfolio. When the fund matures, they receive back their initial investment. Capital gains investors receive everything else. However, if there are capital losses, capital shares suffer them, not the income shares.

Although that's essentially how dual funds work, there are complicating details. For example, dual funds generally don't attempt long-term capital gains. Instead, they take short-term gains and plow them back into the fund for benefit of capital gains investors. Usually the fund's expenses are paid as a percentage of income earned by income shares. That would seem to benefit owners of capital shares, except it encourages managers to maximize income. Sometimes income shares are guaranteed a rate of return, and sometimes not. Sometimes income shares and capital shares have different maturities. Sometimes income shares can be traded for capital shares and vice versa. Sometimes income shares have a set maturity value that is less than their purchase price.

In short, dual funds aren't as uniform in characteristics and consequences as other investments. Their particulars must be examined more carefully. The first American dual funds were issued in 1967, and many of them will be maturing within the next few years. No doubt we are about to see more research about these investments, and perhaps more dual funds will be offered actively to the general public if results are favorable.

For the time being, small investors should be aware that closed-end investment companies, including dual funds, offer outlets for investment. They may not be as convenient and easy to follow as their open-ended counterparts, and as of the present they don't offer many advantages offered by mutual funds. It's probably true that the small investor is better off for now in an open-end mutual fund. But closed-ends bear watching to see if changes in structure and operation make them more desirable.

Even though closed-ends may be of use to small investors, open-ends can be decisively important. They are a means of indirect ownership of corporate and government securities that overcome nearly all the disadvantages of owning securities directly.

SUMMARY

In conclusion, let's lump mutual funds together and review their advantages and disadvantages.

First, mutual funds offer the investor of limited means a broad portfolio of stocks and bonds. That is, they offer diversification.

Second, mutual funds offer professional management.

Third, they offer the chance to make additional investments easily, regularly, and without commissions (except where loads apply).

Fourth, they provide for reinvestment or the opportunity to receive regular payments from the fund.

Fifth, they allow investors to purchase fractional shares.

Sixth, mutual funds offer extraordinary array of investment objectives.

Seventh, they offer many services and conveniences—record-keeping, checking, automatic deposits and withdrawals, bank wire, and sometimes free investment information.

Eighth, fund families offer switch privileges that permit restructuring an entire portfolio in minutes.

Now for disadvantages.

Some funds charge fees and loads that reduce the amount invested.

You don't have a voice in management of a portfolio.

You are subject to all standard investment risks associated with stocks and bonds.

With those considerations in mind, it's time to examine a special type of mutual fund that can be of exceptional value to small investors: money market funds.

Money Market Funds

Money market funds—also called money market mutual funds, MMMFs, or 3MFs—are pools of capital drawn from many investors to buy financial instruments few could afford individually. Although commonly offered by mutual fund families and brokerages, money fund deposits are also available from commercial banks, S&Ls, and credit unions. Holdings of money funds are *money market instruments*—commercial paper from corporations, repurchase agreements from banks and brokerages, bankers acceptances, jumbo CDs from money center banks, and T-bills.

MONEY FUND FEATURES

Because money market instruments are short term, their returns and returns from the money fund buying them fluctuate with market conditions, rising as short-term rates rise and falling as they fall. Short-term rates are volatile and unpredictable, so it's important you subscribe to a money fund with a *constant-dollar share price.*

Constant-dollar share price means the money fund's net asset value is pegged at $1 through techniques approved by the SEC. Unlike fluctuating net asset value of stock and bond funds, money funds hold a constant share price of $1. Send $1,000 to a money fund, and you buy 1,000 shares. Interest your $1,000 earns will vary, but your $1,000 will always be there if you pick a fund that maintains a constant-dollar net asset value. Money fund yields varied from 5 percent to more than 17 percent in the past 10 years, yet share price of constant-dollar funds has remained at $1.

Mutual fund families offer money market funds in minimums of $500 to $10,000, with $1,000 and $2,500 being most frequent minimums for initial investment. Some funds—such as Alliance Capital Reserves[1]—prescribe no minimum initial investment. With most funds, minimums for subsequent investment range from $25 to $500, with $100 and $250 being common. Virtually all are no-load funds.

The comprehensive source for money market funds is *William E. Donoghue's Complete Money Market Guide.*[2] The *Guide* lists hundreds of money funds, including addresses, phone numbers, and investment data about each one.

In selecting a money fund, call for a prospectus from the offering fund family. You'll want to review the fund's performance and call the toll-free number to inquire about current yield. Investigate minimums for initial and subsequent investments, picking the fund that accommodates your ability to invest. However, two considerations are especially important in reviewing the prospectus. They are average portfolio maturity and investment quality.

Average portfolio maturity is the arithmetic mean of the summed maturity dates of the fund's entire portfolio. This is an important figure because the average portfolio maturity shows how close the fund is to a completely cash position. This figure is available weekly in *The Wall Street Journal* and continually from fund representatives via a toll-free number.

The second consideration is quality of the money fund's portfolio. Investments contained in a money fund are rated for quality by independent agencies. These agencies change labels of their ratings, so at various times varying grades may be A or P or A+ or Pl or something completely different. Generally, the prospectus will simply say "The fund invests only in obligations rated this-and-that by so-and-so, an independent rating

---

[1]140 Broadway, New York City 10005 (phone: 800-221−5672).
[2]New York: Harper & Row, 1981.

agency." Or more directly, "The fund invests only in the top three grades of commercial paper."

TYPES OF MONEY FUNDS

There are three types of funds, all available in constant-dollar investments from fund families.

First, a general-purpose money fund, the type we've been talking about, invests in corporate, bank, and government obligations where it finds the highest rates consistent with safety. General-purpose funds usually offer the highest yields, they're safe, and are the kind most frequently advertised.

The second type of money fund invests exclusively in U.S. government and agency securities. Yields on government funds often are a bit below general-purpose funds, yet they offer indirect ownership of government securities with all the safety we learned those investments hold.

A third type of money fund invests in municipal securities for income exempt from federal income tax. As with direct ownership of municipal securities, tax advantages offered by tax-exempt money funds depend upon the individual investor's tax bracket. Income from tax-exempt money funds is taxable by states and municipalities, with possible exception of interest from securities issued by your state.

Interest from money funds is paid monthly. You may have interest reinvested in shares or mailed to you by check. In general, interest from money funds is taxable as "dividends" even though it isn't a dividend. Again, the advantage money funds hold over government or municipal bond funds is stability of principal. The NAV of government and municipal bond funds will fluctuate with interest rates. In contrast, with money funds the NAV remains constant and interest paid will fluctuate.

If you subscribe to a money fund through a mutual fund family, you are entitled to switch privileges, telephone and wire withdrawals, automatic deposit or withdrawals, reinvestment in additional shares or payment to you, record-keeping services, and other conveniences.

Money market funds issue checks to shareholders, much as

depository institutions provide checks in demand deposit accounts. Typically, funds require checks to be written in a minimum of $250 or $500 and also allow a limited number of check withdrawals without charge, so they're no substitute for NOWs and conventional checking accounts.

Every full-service brokerage house has a money market fund. One variant of money funds offered by brokerages is the *cash management account* or CMA. These money funds are offered as an adjunct to brokerage services. Typically, a broker will open a CMA into which dividends from stocks, interest from bonds, and proceeds from sale of securities will be reinvested and from which funds can be withdrawn to buy securities. CMAs offer other services, such as checking, credit cards, and lines of credit. Cash management accounts usually require no minimum for checks and impose no limit on number of checks written.

CMAs are offered mostly by full-service brokerages that charge higher commissions for securities transactions, and typically you must have at least $20,000 in cash and securities to open a CMA. However, discount broker Carl Schwab & Company offers a CMA with no fees and a $1,000 initial investment.

MONEY FUNDS AND DEPOSITORY INSTITUTIONS

With insight and benefit of our earlier chapters, it's easy to see why money market funds give banks fits. They are a combination checking and savings account with no fees, immediate liquidity, and market-level interest. Money funds have no minimum holding period as do time deposits, and there are no penalties for early withdrawals because there's no such thing as an early withdrawal with money funds. Nonetheless, money funds are no substitute for a depository institution.

Let's recap advantages of money funds.

First, money funds offer a constant-dollar investment, like savings accounts, time deposits, and certificates of deposit. They eliminate market risk, and there are no fees to start an account.

Second, money funds that buy government and agency securities have all the safety that government securities imply.

Third, mutual fund families allow investors to put IRA contributions into money funds, as we'll see in the next chapter.

Fourth, money funds generally pay higher interest than do deposit accounts, and they are immediately liquid.

Fifth, some money funds offer tax-exempt returns. However, conventional money funds do yield fully taxable income.

Sixth, money funds offer checking features.

SUMMARY

Investing in a money fund is an excellent first choice for the small investor. It's a great way to wet your financial feet in an investment that offers simplicity and familiarity of a savings/ checking account, introduces you to long-distance investing, acquaints you with principles of mutual funds, and prepares your confidence for more adventurous investments.

CHAPTER TEN

Individual Retirement Accounts and Other Retirement-Anticipation Investments

An individual retirement account (IRA) is an account contributed to by individuals who want to invest for their retirement. IRAs are offered by depositaries, brokerages, mutual funds, and money-management institutions. Each year, investors contribute earned income (unearned income may not be deposited in an IRA) and when they retire they may begin receiving payments from the IRA to supplement social security, pensions, and investment or job income.

Throughout the first half of the 1980s, more than 24 million Americans contributed billions of dollars to individual retirement accounts. IRAs were among the most successful and popular of all personal investments because they offered two tax and investment advantages for nearly all working Americans: all contributions to an IRA were deductible from taxable income, and returns generated by those contributions grew tax free until the worker retired.

For most working Americans and for three quarters of investors who own IRAs, those twin advantages still apply. But following the 1986 tax reform, millions of working Americans and one quarter of current IRA contributors have been forced to reconsider whether IRAs belong in their retirement plans, and a goodly number are concluding that other retirement-anticipation investments are more advantageous.

IRAs REVIEWED

Tax reform preserved two advantages to IRAs. So long as you're a wage earner below age 70½, you can still contribute 100 percent of earned income up to $2,000 ($2,250 for married couples with one wage earner) in an IRA, and future contributions and money in *existing* IRAs continue to grow tax deferred.

Therefore, nothing in the new laws prevents your having an IRA, contributing annually, and earning tax-deferred interest, dividends, and capital gains. Through an IRA you can establish a long-term investment program, possibly reduce taxable income, and defer taxes on your returns. Those are powerful incentives, but they're no longer uniform for all wage earners because ability to deduct IRA contributions from taxable income has been revised. Under the new laws, you can deduct all IRA contributions only if you meet one of two requirements.

First, neither you nor your spouse can be covered by an employer's pension, retirement, or profit sharing plan. Second, if you or your spouse is covered, your adjusted gross income must be less than $25,000 for single taxpayers and $40,000 for couples filing jointly. Under either of these two circumstances, your IRA contribution is fully deductible.

For incomes between $25,000 and $35,000 ($40,000 to $50,000 for couples), your IRA deduction is graduated, eventually reaching a top minimum deduction of $200. (To determine if you can deduct all, part, or none of your IRA contributions, consult the accompanying box.)

Apart from reduced tax attractiveness, new administrative complexities, and an abundance of competing retirement-anticipation investments, there are other reasons why investors are looking skeptically at IRAs.

If you withdraw money from an IRA before reaching age 59½ or becoming permanently disabled, you pay a hefty tax penalty and the withdrawal is immediately and fully taxable. Illiquidity propels younger investors away from IRAs because contributions must be regarded as lifetime investments.

(Actually, that description refers more to the attitude you must adopt than to the law. Investment firms have compared premature withdrawal penalties against tax-deferred returns and determined ranges within which you may withdraw contributions to advantage prematurely. But IRAs are legislated for

CAN YOU DEDUCT IRA CONTRIBUTIONS FROM TAXABLE INCOME?

Permission to deduct IRA contributions partially or fully from taxable income depends upon your adjusted gross income (AGI) and whether you or your spouse is covered by an employer-sponsored retirement program.

Adjusted gross income (AGI) is defined as total income minus personal exclusions *before* taking an IRA deduction.

You're covered by a qualified retirement plan if an employer offers one to you or your spouse even if neither of you is vested. Once eligible, you or your spouse are considered covered even if you choose not to participate. If you're too recently employed to contribute to your employer's plan, you're defined as not covered. But if during the tax year you or your spouse were eligible for a previous employer's plan or will become eligible for a present employer's plan, you're defined as covered.

You May Take a Full IRA Deduction *IF* You Are . . .

- Single with an AGI below $25,000, even if covered by an employer plan.
- Married and filing jointly with combined AGI below $40,000, even if one spouse is covered by an employer plan.
- Not covered by an employer plan and neither is your spouse, regardless of AGI.

You May Take a Partial IRA Deduction *IF* You Are . . .

- Single, covered by employer retirement, and report AGI of $25,000 to $35,000.
- Married and filing jointly, covered by employer retirement, and report AGI between $40,000 and $50,000.
- For each $1,000 of adjusted gross income above $25,000 for singles ($40,000 for couples), your maximum deduction for IRA contributions is reduced by $200. For example, single persons with AGI of $31,000 may deduct $800 from taxable income after an IRA contribution of $2,000. For couples a $46,000 AGI merits a $2,800 deduction on a $4,000 IRA contribution.

You May Not Claim Any IRA Deduction *IF* You Are . . .

- Single, earning more than $35,000, and covered by an employer retirement plan.
- Married and filing jointly, report AGI above $50,000, and you or your spouse is covered by an employer retirement plan.

---

accumulating retirement income. Circumventing that purpose breeches investment discipline and invites Congress to revise IRAs more severely. If you open an IRA believing you can withdraw if you need money, you have the wrong perspective.)

The second disadvantage to IRAs ties in with the first: IRAs may not be used as collateral, under forfeiture of tax advantages.

In addition, IRA contributions now must under some conditions be coordinated with other retirement-anticipation programs. Contributing to an IRA sometimes reduces tax-deductible participation in competing vehicles, and vice versa. This is an important point if you've changed jobs during 1987 or if you're considering a job change. If you're in this situation, seek tax and investment counsel before making retirement-investment decisions, because the new rules are not clear cut.

What with millions of workers having their IRA deductibility reduced or eliminated and with all investors confounded by new frustrations of the Reagan administration, you might think IRAs are doomed. Not entirely.

Three quarters of IRA contributors are not affected by most of the new laws—or so Congress has said. For another thing, self-directed IRAs do offer the broadest assortment of investment choices plus personal control of funds, and that combination adds up to high-potential performance. If you're a savvy investor, top performance in a tax-deferred account is an inducement to keep supporting your IRA.

IS AN IRA FOR YOU?

In determining whether an IRA is still for you, advisers emphasize one point: If you have an IRA now, don't close it. Tax-deferred compounding continues, and closing it will generate tax penalties. If you have several IRAs, do consolidate them under one custodian to reduce fees.

That said, let's look generally at other matters.

As a general rule, wage earners below age 30 will receive greater benefit from conventional investments. Most workers in that age-group haven't many tax incentives compelling contributions to an IRA, and they have many productive decades in which to anticipate retirement. Conversely, investors nearer to age 59½ look favorably upon an IRA because they're closer to eligibility for withdrawal and to retirement.

Before contributing to an IRA, investors should have liquid reserves for emergencies. Depending upon age, indebtedness, and personal circumstances, that reserve may equal 10 to 50 percent of net yearly income. Without this reserve, consider less than a maximum $2,000 IRA contribution.

In addition, evaluate other economic circumstances before contributing to an IRA. A 40-year-old steelworker would be advised to contemplate the tenuousness of employment before making an investment inaccessible as an IRA.

Further, investors should realize that other investments carry some advantages of an IRA while overcoming some of the IRA's disadvantages. For instance, municipal bond funds pay interest exempt from federal tax, and they are liquid if needed. Annuities, discussed in the next chapter, can also defer taxation for many years. More about these considerations in a moment.

Finally, examine an IRA in companion with retirement programs by employers. The wage earner whose employer offers meager retirement benefits will give greater consideration to an IRA, regardless of whether contributions are deductible.

With these generalities acknowledged, let's answer two questions: "Who should start an IRA?" and "Who should continue funding an IRA?"

Employees earning less than $25,000 ($40,000 if married filing jointly) and employees not covered by retirement plans are best advised to initiate or to continue an IRA because they receive full deductibility of contributions and tax-deferred growth. Like all investors, they must assess IRAs against competing vehicles, but circumstances most favor this group of IRA investors.

If you're eligible for partial deduction of contributions, an IRA is less attractive today, but today's contributions will be more attractive if tax rates increase in the future.

At today's lower top tax rates, tax offsets of partially deductible contributions are lessened, but if tax rates increase—which observers regard as likely—eventual aftertax effects of today's partially deductible contributions will be greater. Similarly, today's tax-deferred growth is not as attractive as when tax rates were higher, but attractiveness will increase if tax rates rise.

If you're ineligible to deduct IRA contributions, continuing to fund an IRA probably is not worthwhile unless you're generating great performance in your IRA and can afford nondeductible contributions. True, your nondeductible contributions will grow tax deferred, but other investments can do more. They offer tax-deferred growth *plus* advantages unmatched by IRAs. Those advantages include larger (sometimes deductible) contributions, federally untaxed compounding, no withdrawal penalties, loan provisions or improved accessibility if you need funds before retirement, and greater flexibility.

ALTERNATIVES TO IRAs

One serious alternative to an IRA is a 401(k) plan, which is offered by about 70 percent of the nation's larger companies. The 401(k) permits you to contribute up to $7,000 yearly in an employer-sponsored program, far greater than $2,000 for an IRA. Contributions grow tax deferred and are deposited in your 401(k) *before* you receive them, thereby reducing taxable income and perhaps your tax bracket. Aftertax contributions are also permitted, although there's little reason to put taxable income into a 401(k).

All 401(k) plans permit qualified emergency withdrawals, and employers must offer at least four investment choices for your contributions. Higher contribution levels, accessibility of contributions, tax-deferred growth, and tax-reduced income make 401(k) plans preferable to IRAs for workers whose employers offer them.

Highly attractive to employees of small firms, the Simplified Employee Pension (SEP) lets you contribute up to $7,000 yearly in pretax income to the plan. Pretax contributions lower taxable income, and contributions compound tax deferred.

Keogh plans for self-employed persons and anyone earning income outside a regular job remain among the most advantaged retirement vehicles following tax reform. An estimated one working American in eight earns income from part-time employment beyond a paycheck job, and if you're among them, look into a Keogh. After adjusting reportable income by the amount of the Keogh contribution, you may contribute 20 percent of yearly net self-employment income to a maximum $30,000 in a Keogh. Contributions are excluded from taxable income and grow tax deferred.

Eligibility for IRAs, Keoghs, SEPs, and 401(k)s is determined by your employment and salary. But annuities are retirement-anticipation investments available to anyone, have unlimited contributions, and feature tax-deferred growth.

As we'll see in the next chapter, conventional annuities sponsored by insurance companies or affiliates let you contribute affordable (but not deductible) amounts that grow tax deferred until you retire. As with employment-related retirement vehicles, a penalty is charged for withdrawals before you reach age 59½.

However, the big news is single-premium and variable-premium *life annuities*, which could replace other retirement-anticipation investments.

Single-premium life annuities require you to deposit a single sum, usually at least $5,000. The variable-premium product calls for a series of deposits (usually at least $300 yearly). In both cases, you select among stock, bond, and money market funds for your contributions. Although not deducted from taxable income, contributions are unlimited and grow untaxed until you retire, and account fees are rare.

Single-premium annuities carry insurance coverage, providing an extra underpinning to your retirement program. Variable-premium annuities usually pay death benefits that equal the greater of your account value or your total contributions. Neither insurance coverage nor protection against capital loss is available through other retirement investments we've covered.

In addition, both products offer untaxable, low-interest

or no-interest policy loans without tax penalty—overcoming IRAs's illiquidity—and all investors can contribute to personal annuities along with other retirement investments.

Don't forget municipal bonds as retirement-anticipation investments. Although purchases aren't deductible, most municipals pay federally untaxed—not merely tax-deferred—interest, and some states don't tax interest on their bonds. Even if you're not in the highest tax brackets, you can take advantage of federally untaxed municipal bond interest to accumulate retirement capital.

Whereas direct purchase of municipals usually requires a $5,000 minimum outlay, bond funds are available with initial investments of $1,000 to $5,000 and subsequent investments of $100 to $500. Interest from municipal bond funds (but not capital gains) is also federally untaxed, not merely tax deferred. For investors placing $2,000 yearly or less into a retirement kitty and for investors seeking a supplement to a retirement plan, municipal bond funds are the best choice.

Apart from federally untaxed interest, municipals and municipal funds offer immediate liquidity if you need money. You don't have to request loans, demonstrate emergency need, or suffer withdrawal penalties. This makes them preferable over IRAs for younger investors and ideal supplements to other retirement investments for all workers.

Zero coupon municipal bonds are exceptional retirement investments because they provide federally untaxed interest, predictable accumulations, and a range of maturities. You buy municipal zeros at a price below par value (nearly always $1,000). The difference between purchase price and par value is federally untaxed accreted interest. You can sell zeros any time without explanation, paperwork, or tax penalties, and you needn't coordinate purchases with contributions to other retirement plans. Typically, you buy zeros in units of 10, for an investment of $2,000 to $7,500, price varying inversely to maturity.

IF YOU RETAIN YOUR IRA . . .

Even though many types of retirement-anticipation investments are available to you, you may, for a variety of reasons, want to keep supporting your IRA with deductible or nondeductible contributions. If that's your decision, you must determine your IRA objectives. In building tax-deferred retirement accumulations, investors need to consider capital preservation, income, and growth of capital. Depending upon age and financial circumstances, investors will arrange IRAs to accommodate these three elements.

For example, consider a 35-year-old accountant with marketable job skills and 30 working years ahead of her. This IRA contributor can concentrate on growth. At this stage of life and career, stability of principal is a lesser concern. That's not so for a 55-year-old who anticipates retirement in 10 years. This IRA contributor will be more concerned with investments that preserve principal, yet growth is also important, as he or she may live into his or her 80s.

The general rule for IRAs is "Seek maximum income consistent with preservation of capital." Let's consider ways to achieve capital preservation, income, and capital growth.

WHERE TO PLACE IRA CONTRIBUTIONS

For IRA investors seeking stability of principal, constant-dollar accounts with savings institutions and money funds with brokers or mutual funds fit the ticket. Savings institutions are becoming more innovative with IRA packages, but mostly their IRAs are standard certificates of deposit. You fill out the IRA forms, make the prescribed deposit, and receive a stated rate of interest. With money funds the procedure is the same. Establishment and yearly maintenance fees are usually but not always required for both, and amounts vary with institutions.

The advantage of constant-dollar IRA vehicles is that you'll keep the dollar you contributed while interest compounds. IRAs with savings institutions are backed by governmental agencies, and money market funds investing in government obligations provide maximum protection against loss. Opening an IRA through a bank or money fund is the safest course. Generally you need not invest the maximum $2,000 in these vehicles. Most savings institutions will open an IRA for $500, and money market funds available through fund families have similar minimums.

The disadvantage of IRAs through depositaries and funds is the flipside of their advantages. If the bank promises 8 percent compounded interest, you receive that and no more. Money funds will pay prevailing rates, which have varied from 5 to 17 percent in recent years.

However, IRA investments in stocks and bonds are the best choices for income and capital growth. There are two ways to acquire stocks and bonds for your IRA.

The first way is to buy them directly through a "self-directed IRA" sponsored by a broker. As the term *self-directed* implies, you pick the securities for your IRA, directing a broker to buy or sell for your account. You pay normal commissions and probably start-up and maintenance fees. At present, commissions are included in the maximum $2,000 you can contribute to your IRA. Therefore, if your broker charges $100 in commissions the maximum you can invest is $1,900. If you contribute more than $2,000 to an IRA, the overage is subject to continuing tax penalties.

Maintenance fees can be paid directly or deducted from proceeds in your account, and the broker will reinvest interest and dividends in a money fund to provide further tax-deferred accumulations. If you're willing to pay commissions, you can trade securities in your self-directed IRA at will.

Because capital losses from IRAs aren't deductible, some advisers suggest concentrating IRA holdings in bonds and high-yielding stocks rather than growth stocks.

Purchase of bonds through a self-directed IRA makes sense. Novice investors can pick bonds with more assurance than stocks, and to the extent anything is certain in investment, individual bonds offers safety, income, and capital appreciation. Government bonds (EE and HH bonds excepted) are suitable for IRAs. Do not purchase municipal bonds for your IRA. Interest which otherwise would be federally tax exempt will be fully taxed when you begin receiving payments from your IRA. Including munies in your IRA merely converts untaxed income into taxed income.

Especially popular IRA investments are zero coupon bonds and zero coupon certificates of deposit. We noted that zeros pay no coupon interest but instead sell at deep discounts from par, the difference between purchase price and maturity value being accrued interest. Zeros offer four advantages for IRAs. First, they can be purchased without commissions if you compare brokers. Second, they often are designed expressly for IRA accounts, meaning you can buy them in even multiples totaling $2,000. Third, zeros lock in a known interest rate if held to par, so you know exactly how much you'll have when they mature. Fourth, zero CDs and government bonds assembled by brokerages as zeros are highly safe investments.

In addition to purchasing stocks and bonds for IRAs directly, investors can own them indirectly through mutual funds. Virtually every mutual fund family offers IRA accounts, and maintenance fees are less than those charged by full-service brokers.

Advantages to the mutual fund IRA include diversification and professional management. You also can switch investments in fund families among mutual funds as you see fit. Most fund families allow a maximum number of cost-free switches each year. Refer back to Chapter Eight for a refresher on switch privileges.

Whether you choose direct or indirect IRA investments, your portfolio can be arranged to accommodate capital preservation, income, and capital growth, and the portfolio can be rearranged as desired. Bear in mind that you can transfer IRA monies from, say, a time certificate to a mutual fund or to a self-directed IRA. So long as you don't personally hold money en route from one IRA account to another for longer than 60 days, you'll not encounter tax problems.

Besides conventional IRAs, there are two other types: spousal IRAs and IRA rollovers.

The spousal IRA is for the increasingly rare case of households in which only one spouse works outside the home. The employed spouse may contribute up to $2,250 in IRA accounts, not more than $2,000 of which may be deposited in any single account.

IRA rollovers accommodate transfers from retirement accounts established by an employer to an individual account. Workers vested in employer-sponsored retirement programs may transfer amounts contributed by their employer to a rollover if they change jobs. Rollovers are similar to conventional IRAs, with two exceptions: (1) a rollover is a one-time deposit which cannot be added to; (2) only amounts contributed by *employers* may be deposited.

After receiving a retirement distribution from a former employer, you have 60 days to deposit the employer's contribution in a rollover. Portions you contributed to a former employer's retirement program are yours to keep, and there is no additional tax liability because you've already paid tax on income you contributed to the program. If you fail to meet the 60-day deadline, the employer's contribution becomes fully taxable current income. Investments suited for conventional IRAs are appropriate for rollovers.

SUMMARY

An IRA can be a highly desirable way to anticipate retirement even though a growing number of investments offer the small investor a tax credit and tax-advantaged accumulations. The proliferation of investments available for IRA contributions makes possible high returns, convenience, and lots of money. However, retirement-minded investors want to consider other tax-advantaged investments, and one of those—annuities—is the subject of the next chapter.

CHAPTER ELEVEN

Annuities, Tax-Deferred, and Tax-Advantaged Investments

Among the goals of investing is to receive the highest aftertax return on your money. We've talked about overattention to tax minimizing (i.e., failure to receive maximum posttax income by trying to escape taxes) but you want investing to pay off for you and not the tax collector. The best of all worlds would be one in which you could invest for maximum return and disregard taxes. The second-best would be that in which you could invest for maximum return and postpone taxes. This latter possibility is available through annuities and tax-deferred investments.

An annuity is a contract, usually with an insurance company, which allows you to invest current income in exchange for future income. During the period your investment grows, you pay no taxes on its returns. When you cash the annuity in or when the date for withdrawals is reached, your accrued earnings are taxable at rates determined by your total income.

The amount contributed to an annuity, the rate of interest earned, and the length of time the annuity is allowed to grow are the three important considerations of an annuity contract.

First, amount contributed.

TYPES OF ANNUITIES

Annuities are of two general types: those requiring a relatively large one-time deposit and those allowing smaller deposits paid over many periods. Although annuities go by many names, the former is usually called a *fixed premium annuity* and the latter a *variable-premium annuity*. The term *premium* is a clue to the insurance affiliation of most annuities. The condition is "most annuities" because there is a *private annuity*, which involves a temporary disposition of high-value, income-producing assets and is established through legal counsel.

The advantage to the fixed premium annuity is that the initial deposit ($5,000 or more) accrues more interest immediately. The disadvantage is the size of the initial investment. The advantage of the variable-premium annuity is that investors can set aside smaller amounts ($25 to $100) as convenient without denting budgets or other investments. Disadvantages are that variable-premium annuities sometimes pay less interest than fixed premiums and it takes longer to accumulate a critical investment mass via small accumulations.

Second, rate of interest earned.

Annuities often pay a guaranteed minimum rate of interest (4 percent is common) plus a rate determined by market conditions and wisdom of their investment managers. In mid-1987, many annuities pay 7 to 8 percent—a figure 1 predictable percent less than rates on long-term corporate and government bonds, the main investments of annuity managers.

Although that interest rate may sound low, remember that this interest is accumulating tax free. Therefore, taxable equivalent yield is a more significant consideration than nominal rate of interest. Taxable equivalent yield is determined by your personal income tax bracket.

Third, length of accumulation.

An annuity is a contract in which one party (the issuer) agrees to provide another (the owner or annuitant) a rate of interest for a specified period. That period is agreed upon by both parties. You can start an annuity today and begin receiving payments next month, or you can start an annuity today and wait 30 years or more before withdrawal.

Annuities are most useful in a long-term program of tax-deferred accruals wherein interest grows without tax. At 8 percent interest a fixed premium annuity of $10,000 will grow to more than $100,000 in 30 years, and over the same period a yearly investment of $1,000 will grow to more than $122,000.

Annuities can be highly useful for small investors wishing to accumulate a retirement nest egg, and that's one of their chief uses. They are also excellent supplements to an IRA, and they're suited to any long-term savings intention, such as buying a house, anticipating college tuition, planning a world cruise, or just accumulating tax-deferred returns on unneeded cash.

SOURCES OF ANNUITIES

Because an annuity is a long-term contract, it's wise to check the financial stability of the sponsoring insurance company. Most offering companies are well capitalized, and annuity investments are considered highly safe. The best source for checking financial strength of an insurance company's annuity is A. M. Best Co., whose informative *Best's Insurance Report*[1] is available at most libraries.

SPECIFICATIONS

In completing the annuity contract, you must first specify the designated annuitant, the person to whom annuity payments will be made. That may be you, your spouse, or another person in whom you have insurable interest, such as a grandchild or business partner.

Next, you must prescribe who owns the annuity contract. This is important because the owner of the annuity may change the annuitant. Usually the annuitant is the owner.

You also specify the date on which payments from the annuity begin. You don't always have to pick an annuity commencement date at the time of purchase, and it may be changed later anyway.

Other details may or may not need completing, such as any special instructions you wish observed.

Perhaps most important, you must specify the manner in which you wish proceeds from your investment distributed to

---

[1] If volume is not available, write A. M. Best, A. M. Best Road, Oldwick, New Jersey 08858 (phone number: 201-439-2200).

the annuitant on the annuity commencement date. Typically, you have three or four choices:

1. Lump Sum Distribution. All accrued interest plus principal mailed to the annuitant in a single check.
2. Period Certain. Accumulated proceeds distributed over a set period, frequently 120 or 240 months.
3. Lifetime Receipts. The "straight life" annuity pays a certain amount for life of the annuitant.
4. Joint and Survivor Payments. The annuity provides income for the life of the annuitant and a survivor of insurable interest.
5. Some Combination of Any Above. For example, large lump-sum payment coupled with a period certain, or a period certain in companion with lifetime receipts.

Different annuities offer some, but not all, of these choices, and investors must look carefully at payment options when investigating annuities. Note this well: you usually need not specify a payment option when you purchase an annuity, but once you select an option you usually cannot change it.

ANNUITY PAYMENTS

A cursory review of payment choices above would suggest that, for example, an annuity contract promising to pay a period certain would be able to provide higher income than an annuity promising to pay lifetime income. The longer the period of payment, the lower is the promised amount of payment to you. You trade higher payments for a shorter period of guaranteed payment, and vice versa.

Just as we classed annuities according to fixed or variable *premiums* that you pay to the offering organization, so can they be classified according to fixed or variable *payments* to you.

A *fixed payment annuity* pays the annuitant a fixed amount for a contracted period. Managers of the annuity's portfolio look over their investment options, confer with actuaries who measure life expectancy, and compare findings with the annuitant's preference for income. Because everyone proceeds from established figures—prevailing yields on fixed-income securities, relatively uniform life demographics, and the annuitant's contracted length of income stream—the insurance company and the annuitant can compute payments with acceptable accuracy. The advantage to such an arrangement is relative certainty and predictability of income. The disadvantage is that contractual payments may not be sufficient for annuitants' needs.

In an attempt to overcome this disadvantage, insurance companies some years ago developed *variable income annuities*. As we noted, most annuities invest in fixed-income securities such as government and corporate bonds. This ensures predictable returns and minimizes surprises. However, variable income annuities invest some portion of your funds in equity investments. Payments you receive are in some measure determined by fluctuations in value of stocks within the annuity's portfolio. "Some measure" is an important qualifier because typically a portion of the variable income annuity portfolio will remain in bonds, which provide a floor of predictable returns.

The idea behind variable income annuities is to provide potentially higher income to annuitants, the assumption being that stocks outperform bonds, while establishing a base level of returns from bonds.

Whatever form your annuity payments take and for whatever period, income from annuities is fully taxable as current income, although returns of invested capital aren't taxed because you've already paid taxes on income contributed to the annuity. Occasionally you will hear the terms *tax deferred annuity* and *income annuity*. The former is an annuity in its accumulation phase, when returns are building untaxed; the latter is an annuity in its payout phase, when it's providing current income.

Selecting a payout option is a difficult point on which to advise. Some of us fear outliving our income and choose the lifetime annuity in exchange for lower current income. Others find some satisfaction in providing for heirs and want the survivor option. Still others who have additional income prefer the higher payments of a period certain, relying upon other investments for support should they outlive their contract with the insurance company. And a few will want a lump-sum payment in order to buy a retirement condo or a long-postponed world cruise.

PAYMENT CONSIDERATIONS

In deciding upon a choice of payment, three considerations prevail: anticipated tax status on the annuity commencement date, level of income provided by other investments as part of total income needed to maintain a desired standard of living, and intended use of the accumulated money.

In choosing a payout option, you'd be wise to consult a book, *Successful Investing*,[2] by the staff of United Business Service. It has an excellent chapter on annuities, and its extended discussion of other investments is well worth reading.

Annuities are a superb means for the small investor to build tax-deferred income safely and conveniently, but there's always The First Dictum to remember. In this case, the advantages of annuities were so accessible that Congress moved to prevent "abuses" of this convenient investment vehicle by building in a few tax disadvantages.

The apparent intent of these legislative changes is to prevent people from accumulating idle funds without paying Uncle Sam his due. If you make withdrawals from an annuity fewer than 10 years old you'll pay 10 percent of the amount withdrawn as a tax penalty to the government unless you're at least 59½ years old. Unlike the interest penalty for premature withdrawal from time deposits, the interest penalty for withdrawals from annuities isn't deductible from federal income tax. This provision applies to withdrawals of funds from the annuity during its accumulation phase, not to payments received starting with the commencement date.

The second provision reinterprets the nature of the income received from your annuity on the commencement date. In the past, annuities were presumed to return investors' contributed principal before paying anything from accumulated interest. That is, the first amounts contributed were presumed to be the

---

[2]New York: Simon & Schuster, 1983.

first amounts disbursed. More than likely, that returned principal had been contributed from taxed income, so under the old system an annuity's first several payments were a return of previously taxed income and not subject to additional taxation as current income. No more. Now annuities are presumed to pay previously untaxed accumulated interest first and to return principal later.

The chief consequence of changes in tax statutes is to enforce annuities as long-term savings, and 10 years is the operative definition of long term. In other words, if you contribute to an annuity, you'd better be prepared to leave the money in place for a decade or face the unpleasant tax consequences if you're younger than 59½ years old.

In addition, some annuities—especially those sponsored by mutual funds—levy surrender charges for withdrawals prior to the annuity commencement date in addition to tax penalties imposed by Uncle Sam. Those charges can be as much as 5 percent of *principal* contributed, with a downward-sliding scale usually applying. Further, mutual fund-affiliated annuities have administrative fees for early withdrawals, usually $10 to $50, and the same is true of annuities contracted through brokerages.

This is a double whammy. By withdrawing funds from your annuity prematurely you lose principal and interest. The point bears repeating: regard an annuity as a long-term investment. Don't buy annuities with emergency savings, or taxes and charges will eat your funds faster than Pac-Man devours dots. Ask about fees, charges, and taxes before investing.

Further, don't invest in annuities with untaxed income. For example, don't purchase an annuity with proceeds from municipal bonds or municipal bond funds. By doing so you convert federally untaxed income into income that will be taxed.

FOREIGN ANNUITIES AND ROLLOVERS

In closing discussion of conventional annuities we should be aware that foreign insurance companies, particularly in Switzerland, offer annuities. An advantage to investing outside the United States is that foreign currencies may appreciate against the dollar, thereby increasing returns to you when you reconvert the currency into dollars upon receiving payments. A disadvantage is that premiums must be paid in the currency of ultimate repayment. If the exchange rate of the currency of repayment increases, your dollar-valued premiums increase during the annuity's accumulation phase. If you're interested in a foreign annuity, the Swiss are a logical preference. One company dealing with Americans is:

Assurex, S.A.
Volkmarstrasse 10
P.O. Box 209
8033 Zurich
Switzerland

Besides conventional deferred annuities, many mutual funds offer rollover annuities, often called *guaranteed return plans*. Through these vehicles investors obtain a guaranteed rate of interest to accumulate tax deferred for a specified time, usually a year, and that rate of interest is usually higher than interest for conventional annuities. Advantages are threefold: a high rate of return (around 8.5 percent in 1987) guaranteed for a period, tax-deferred compounding, and security of interest and principal associated with conventional annuities. Typically, minimum initial investment is $5,000.

Guaranteed return plans are *rollovers* because at end of the contracted accumulation period the deposit plus deferred interest can be recontracted, or rolled over, extending tax-deferred accumulation. When rolling over the deposit, you might receive a lower rate of interest.

Identical tax consequences and fees or charges applying to standard annuities also pertain to guaranteed return plans. Even though these products are advertised as short-term, tax-deferred accumulation vehicles, you have to treat them as long-term investments or pay the consequences.

As the fine print testifies, sponsors of these programs expect you to hang around. Most, for instance, stagger surrender charges, encouraging you to keep cash on account five years. Some permit you to withdraw a portion of your deposit each year without surrender fee, an option usually flecked by an asterisk plunging you to the back of the prospectus wherein are annotated unsavory tax consequences of doing so.

Guaranteed return plans can be useful to three categories of investors who can fork over the minimum initial investment.

First, they can be useful to people within a few years of retirement. Say you've accumulated a nugget from a lifetime of investing. You can place that sum into a guaranteed return plan and draw tax-deferred interest higher than prevailing rates on similar investments and protected from fluctuations in other markets. They're also useful recepticles for company pensions not needed right away or for other lump-sum disbursements from insurance. Proceeds can be withdrawn after retirement, when your tax bracket is often lower.

Second, guaranteed return plans can be of advantage to investors willing to accept higher accumulated interest now in exchange for the risk of falling interest rates later. Such an investor is the converse of the investor who places his or her annuity into a money fund-affiliated annuity now and hopes interest rates will rise later.

Third, guaranteed return plans are useful to investors who already have an annuity that isn't paying as much interest as the new guaranteed return plan. Section 1035 of the Internal Revenue Code allows untaxed exchanges from one annuity to another. Consult a tax adviser before switching, however.

INSURANCE PRODUCTS

Insurance products have changed more in the past 8 years than in the preceeding 50. Following tax reform in 1986, insurance products have become more advantaged in two senses. First, Congress didn't legislate away the advantages to standard insurance products. Second, the insurance industry added features to long-standing products that compensate for wounds other tax-deferred accounts did suffer under tax reform.

When investigating insurance products, however, you must distinguish between their insurance features and investment features. That's becoming difficult to do because new insurance products offer both features, but also because some insurance companies offer investments independent of their insurance products as well as investments that mate insurance with an investment program. It's becoming common to find insurance companies registered with the National Association of Securities Dealers and selling mutual funds and money market funds as well as conventional life insurance and insurance-investment products.

Earlier in the chapter we saw why single-premium and variable-premium life *annuities* can replace or supplement IRAs, Keoghs, and retirement-anticipation programs. With both products, a portion of your investment buys insurance coverage and with the remainder you select among stock, bond, and money market funds for untaxed capital growth. In addition, both products offer untaxable, low-interest or no-interest policy loans without tax penalty. These products can replace or supplement IRAs because they provide tax-deferred accumulations, overcome IRAs's illiquidity via loan provisions, and insure your life for your heirs.

At this point in our discussion, it will be useful to remind ourselves that long-available insurance policies like whole life build up cash value that can be accessed though low-interest loans. Although not really an *investment*, whole life insurance provides a financial underpinning for your family and can make funds available from its cash buildup.

Whole life is what we typically think of as *life insurance*. That is, you pay premiums to purchase insurance coverage that distributes an untaxable death benefit to your heirs. *Single-premium whole life* is, as the term implies, a situation in which you pay a one-time premium and receive insurance coverage for the remainder of your life. *Variable-premium whole life* requires a series of premium payments for as long as your policy is in force.

In both cases, part of your premiums purchase insurance coverage. But the portion of your premium not needed to cover insurance cost is invested by the insurance company. The returns earned on this "excess" premium accrue in your account as untaxable *cash value*. Over a number of years, cash value can accrue to a tidy sum. If you cancel your policy, cash value is returned to you, but you also forfeit continuing insurance coverage. That's why it's possible for you to borrow against cash value through a low-interest (but not interest-deductible) loan with the insurance company.

The advantages of whole life are many—principal is guaranteed by the insurance company, yields are market level, loans from your policy are not taxable, cash value accretes untaxed, and the insurance feature provides untaxed disbursements to your heirs. Obviously, whole life is not a total investment program, but single-premium and variable-premium products certainly deserve a look.

Single-premium whole life is emerging as an excellent alternative to a uniform gifts to minors account (UGMA) following tax reform. Before 1986, parents could contribute cash or securities to a UGMA registered in the name of their child, and gains from the account were untaxed until the child accrued $1,000 in unearned income, at which time the income would be taxed at the child's lower rates. Because UGMAs are generally used to build a tuition fund, the child usually withdrew accrued income from the UGMA and received a largely untaxed sum when starting college.

Following tax reform, these transfers to children *below age 14* are now taxed on the amount of net unearned income. Net unearned income is defined as unearned income (interest, dividends, capital gains) minus the child's standard deduction ($500) or minus the child's itemized deductions as allowed for producing unearned income. Effectively, a child's net unearned income above $1,000 is now taxed at the parents' rates; net unearned income from $500 to $1,000 is taxed at the child's rate; net unearned income of $500 is reduced to zero by the child's standard deduction and there is no tax liability.

Single-premium whole life diminishes these complications. You can purchase a whole life policy at minimal cost on an infant's life. Cash value buildup accrues untaxed in anticipation of the child's college years. When it comes time to tap the policy for tuition, you can cancel it and receive the cash value, taxed at the child's rates, or you can borrow against cash value, leaving the insurance in force while obtaining funds for college.

Universal life insurance is more akin to the insurance-investment concept that has emerged following tax reform. Although based on long-standing insurance concepts, universal life mates insurance coverage with a "side fund" that's invested in bonds, stocks, or money funds. Universal life comes in single-premium and variable-premium forms, the former requiring a single up-front payment and the latter a series of payments in amounts that will vary over the life of your policy.

With universal life, a portion of the premium pays for insurance coverage and the remainder is invested. Returns from the invested portion accrue federally untaxed. With some offering companies you have control over investment choices; you can place the noninsurance portion of your premium into stocks, bonds, or money funds to take advantage of markets. Other companies don't permit personal control over investment choices.

Universal life permits long-term, tax-free accumulations that can be accessed through policy loans if you need funds. Thus, it is a long-term investment that can have short-term accessibility, but the sales and investment attraction is definitely on the long-term horizon, and that's how you should consider Universal Life.

This is an important point to remember because many insurance companies are promoting the untaxed loan access to cash buildup as a primary inducement. There's no question that this feature can be important. It's possible, for example, to structure loans from a universal life policy to create an income stream each year, effectively treating universal life as a form of annuity created by continually borrowing against your cash buildup. Returns from the side fund pay off interest from the loan, in effect creating federally untaxed income without overt repayment of the debt.

Although attractive, this feature diminishes long-term accumulations and potentially devours the insurance coverage paid to your heirs in the event of your untimely death. In other words, the investment and insurance advantages are not preserved to mutual advantage if you take repeated advantage of loan provisions. This is a point to consider in your deliberations and to discuss with insurance company representatives.

Individual companies offering universal life will provide account summaries that are similar to a prospectus, and these summaries will highlight specific advantages to a particular company's offering. In reading this material prior to investing, you'll want to be concerned with accessibility features, interest rate charged for borrowing, the extent of insurance coverage attendant to the investment aspect of the policy, account and surrender charges, and distinguishing features that separate Company A's policy from Company B's.

With regard to insurance-investment vehicles, we should remember that their advantages exist at the whim of Congress, and Congress has exercised its whims to the disadvantage of tax-deferred investments in the past. For instance, it altered laws pertaining to annuities in 1983–84. Although insurance products remained largely untouched by 1986 tax reform, Congress specifically declared it would review insurance products in 1989, the year after a national election. Politicians like to change tax laws early in their terms to leave voters maximum time to forget, and 1989 would be a good year to do so. Finally, Congress has changed the tax code 19 times in the past 23 years. Sacred cows like IRAs, municipal bonds, annuities, and limited partnerships have been gored by recent tax reform. There's no reason why insurance products can't be next.

Before leaving the subject of tax-deferred investments, remember that several conventional investments offer tax deferral—although post-1986 Congress-watchers are speculating whether tax deferral features will remain after the next presidential election.

Capital gains from directly held stocks and bonds aren't taxed until they're taken. If you buy a stock for $50 and it appreciates to $100, your gain isn't taxed unless you sell the stock. The same is true for any capital appreciation—on gold or silver, for example, as well as for coins, gems, land, or art objects. Income is deferred from taxation until it's claimed, at least under 1987 tax laws.

And there's the EE Savings Bond. Tax on accrued interest can be deferred until you cash the bond, and if you exchange for HH bonds taxable interest can be postponed even longer.

Of course, interest from municipal bonds, munie bond funds, and munie money market funds is exempt from federal tax.

Another tax-deferred investment is a company-sponsored

pension and stock plan. Plans vary with each company, but they can be an excellent way to accrue tax-deferred income. Consult your personnel office about options available to you.

SUMMARY

In sum, small investors have several choices for postponing payment of federal taxes from investing, for investing in tax-exempt or tax-advantaged vehicles, and for displacing taxation to lesser-taxed family members. These options aren't just for the wealthy, and if you have wisdom and discipline, your investments can grow for years through programs that provide more for you and less for the IRS.

Precious Metals

The problem with precious metals is that you have to distinguish among worshiping them, buying them, and investing in them, and that's not easy to do, especially in the case of gold.

The human species reveres gold with a transfixion which defies explanation. People may say they own gold as an investment, but you never know if they're speaking truth or indulging mankind's fixation. Other people grow apoplectic if you even suggest gold is an investment, but for all we know they have a bundle of the stuff under the fireplace. There's no telling why people hold this near-supernatural regard for precious metals—gold, especially—but we can attempt exposition of why people buy or invest in them.

GOLD AS HEDGE

Some people buy gold because they believe it is the only universally accepted currency; others, because it isn't currency at all, which is to say no government has applied ink to paper and called the result a dollar, a mark, or a zloty.

"No matter how cleverly governments assure us that paper and ink are real money, whenever a small but significant percentage of the world's population gets worried, they want gold and silver," writes Howard J. Ruff in *How to Prosper during the Coming Bad Years.*[1]

The key is *worried.* Prices of gold—and to some extent other metals—reflect world events, rising when Russians invade another country or when international banking seems overextended, falling when armies are inactive and bankers stingy. However, this precious metals buyer isn't concerned with price. He figures *his* native currency may become worthless or that apocalypse will make *all* currencies worthless, but that gold will be valued. He's probably right, but if things get that bad he'd better own a cache of food and a shotgun. Nonetheless, some people buy gold from the belief it has intrinsic, universal value and, like any necessity of survival, is cheap at any price.

People buy gold to *insure* other investments. Typically, the price of gold moves inversely to stocks and bonds. When they go down, gold goes up—usually. By holding gold these buyers hope to reduce market risk of paper investments.

People buy gold as a hedge against inflation even though scholarly studies dispute the intelligence of their behavior. The price of gold does rise with the rate of inflation—maybe because people flee to gold as a hedge, or maybe because they know gold's price rises with inflation and buy gold expecting other purchasers to bid up its price. Paradoxically, interest rates rise with inflation, and high-interest rates dampen the price of gold.

GOLD AS INVESTMENT

Use as survival currency, portfolio insurance, and inflation hedge are reasons to buy gold, but there's some question whether buying it for those reasons is *investing.* One invests to receive returns, and metals do so by providing capital appreciation. Those who bought gold at $40 an ounce in the 1970s and watched it soar to $800+ per ounce had handsome gains. Of course, those who bought at $800 aren't happy at 1987's price of $400.

---

[1]New York: Warner Books, 1979.

If you invest in precious metals, you must decide the form in which to do so. Several options are available: (1) owning bullion directly in coins or bars, (2) through certificate programs, (3) stock in mining companies or mutual funds.

Those who buy metals for catastrophe value prefer bullion coins, and they take possession of them. If catastrophe makes gold or silver a medium of exchange, coins will probably be accepted over bullion bars. Coins also provide capital gains as the price of their metal increases.

Many gold coins are available for small investors, the most popular (until the U.S. embargoed importation in 1986) being the South African Krugerrand. In the 1980s, the Canadian Maple Leaf and the Mexican Gold Peso are favored. Even the United States mints gold coins like the American Eagle from time to time. An advantage to governmental coins is that the mining government assures metal content, reducing need to assay the coin. Many silver coins are available, such as the Sunshine.

Gold and silver coins can be purchased through coin dealers or the mail. You walk into the coin shop, pay for the coin, and walk out, or any investment publication will reveal companies selling coins by mail. If you buy coins through the mail you'll pay a delivery charge, and perhaps state taxes.

Purchase of coins has a couple of advantages. You may buy 2-ounce, 1-ounce, ½-ounce, ¼-ounce, and 10th-ounce sizes that accommodate your budget. The price will include per-ounce cost of gold, a 1 to 3 percent dealer's markup, and a minting premium to cover costs of converting gold to specie. For coins containing less than one ounce of metal, minting premiums are higher than for larger coins, meaning you pay more for less gold.

Another advantage to coins is that dealers will usually buy them back, providing liquidity. Dealer's repurchase price will be the per-ounce price of gold minus 1 to 3 percent. Avoid *special series* coins and medallions issued by private mints. Liquidity may be difficult if you wish to sell, and, unlike coins with a government's name on them, quality and metallic content may be suspect.

Gold and silver bullion bars are available in weights of a

kilo to an ounce, although you can buy precious metal wafers (also called *bars* even though they aren't) in sizes less than an ounce. If you buy gold in less than round lots (i.e., 20 one-ounce coins or 1 10-ounce bar) fees may be a considerable percentage of investment.

Some coin shops sell bullion bars, and they may also be purchased through the mail. Commissions, delivery fees, and striking fees will be charged, and safeguarding precious metals adds expenses for a safe deposit box or storage charges with a dealer.

An alternative for those who want bullion but not personal possession is the certificate program. Certificates don't offer the catastrophe value of gold coins, but they're still ownership of gold, and as such they provide opportunity for capital appreciation. The holder of a certificate owns a portion of a larger quantity of gold purchased and held by a broker. Citibank offers a certificate program with a $1,000 minimum investment. Your certificate represents ownership of a specified amount of bullion purchased by Citibank and collected into a common account. Citibank charges commissions to buy and sell and also charges a storage fee after one year. For further information contact:

> Citibank Gold Purchase Plan
> Citibank Gold Center
> 399 Park Avenue
> New York, N.Y. 10043
> (phone: 800-223-1080)

DOLLAR-COST AVERAGING

The long-term way to accumulate precious metal, whether through direct purchase or a certificate program, is by *dollar-cost averaging*. Because the price of metal fluctuates daily, it's difficult to pick highs and lows. You avoid the price problem through dollar-cost averaging, in which you invest a fixed amount—say $50—at fixed periods—say monthly. With regular, fixed investments, your average cost of accumulating gold falls because you buy more when price drops and less as it rises. Consider this example.

	Price of Gold per Ounce	Invest Dollar Cost	Buy (oz.)
January	$ 25	$ 50	2
February	50	50	1
March	10	50	5
April	100	50	0.50
May	200	50	0.25
June	25	50	2
Totals		$300	10.75
Averages		$ 50	1.79

Gold fluctuated between $10 and $200 per ounce in our example. Through dollar-cost averaging, you acquired 10.75 ounces for $300, for an average price of $27.90 per ounce and average accumulation of 1.79 ounces per month. If you'd bought 1.79 ounces per month at prevailing prices, you'd have paid $733.90, an average price of more than $68 per ounce. Dollar-cost averaging is a powerful investment tool, and it works for any investment that fluctuates in price, including stocks and mutual fund shares.

Still, dollar-cost averaging isn't infallible. Note June in the example. You'd invested $300 to acquire 10.75 ounces, and at the price of $25 per ounce your metal is worth $268.75. Dollar-costing won't keep you from losing money, because the problem of selling at the high remains. But it can help you accumulate metal at substantial advantage when the long-term trend is upward.

MINING STOCKS

Like any product, metals are produced by corporations that sell stock. By owning stock in mining companies you have ownership—but not possession—of metal they produce, and you can participate in price increases of their product. Two additional advantages: mining stocks sometimes pay dividends, and precious metals companies mine other metals, diversifying your holdings.

Mining stocks involve the same dilemmas of investing in any stock. Shares in precious metals mining companies are subject to the price volatility of their product, and many of the best-known and widely held mining stocks are in politically unsettled countries, adding international risk to risks associated with equities and metals.

Rather than own shares, you may prefer mutual funds that purchase these shares, diversify your holdings, and provide professional management. Major mutual fund families now offer precious metals funds of many kinds. Two funds that have appeared on many recommended lists are:

> United Services Fund
> 15748 Interstate Highway
> P.O. Box 29467
> San Antonio, Tex. 78229
> (phone: 800–531–5777)

> International Investors, Inc.
> 122 East 42d Street,
> New York, N.Y. 10168
> (phone 800–221–2220)

International Investors, Inc., offers the option of receiving quarterly dividends in gold coins. It combines direct ownership of gold and indirect ownership of stocks.

SILVER AND OTHER METALS

Silver, *poor man's gold*, is a popular metal that may be purchased in coins, bars, wafers, certificates, and shares in mining companies. Many investors buy pre-1965 American dimes and quarters for their silver content. American silver coinage may be purchased singly, in rolls, in half-bags, and full bags at prices ranging between $1 and several thousand.

Silver offers two advantages over gold. It is cheaper—in 1987 about $5 per ounce compared to $400 for gold. Also, silver tends to increase with the price of gold when times are bad and to increase during economic upswing when gold is falling, for it's an industrial metal influenced by industrial activity. On a percentage basis, the price of silver is much more volatile than gold, however.

Platinum, palladium, and other rare or strategic metals are available in much the same fashion as gold and silver. Investing in these esoteric metals is not for the novice or low-stakes investor.

SUMMARY

To lump these metallic possibilities into one summarized alloy we have the following:

Advantages of owning bullion and certificates:

1. Currency of last resort against economic collapse.
2. Insurance against adverse moves by conventional investments.
3. Capital appreciation.

Disadvantages of owning bullion and certificates:

1. Volatile price swings.
2. No dividends or interest.
3. Commissions, premiums, fees, delivery charges, and taxes are higher than for other investments.
4. Metal must be guarded, perhaps costing storage fees.
5. Metals are not normal currency and liquidity may be difficult.

Advantages of owning mining and mutual fund shares:

1. Shares may pay dividends.
2. Opportunity for capital appreciation.
3. Liquidity.
4. Some companies mine other metals, offering diversification.

Disadvantages of owning mining and mutual fund shares:

1. Purchase involves same disadvantages as any stock plus disadvantages associated with precious metals.

Additional Investment Possibilities

We've covered an exceptional array of possibilities open to people with $5,000 or less, but financial markets are constantly providing options and opening wealth to larger numbers of investors. Accordingly, loose investment ends are cropping up faster than they can be tied off. Here are additional investments that don't seem to fit anywhere else.

PRECIOUS GEMS

Diamonds are a girl's best friend, and dogs are man's best friend, and that should settle which is the smarter of the sexes. In the past, investment-grade gems have paid handsome capital appreciation for many investors, but that circumstance hasn't been so rewarding lately.

The uninitiated investor isn't advised to sink money into gems—and that's gems not jewelry. You're even less wise to buy jewelry under the assumption it's an investment. Precious stones don't pay current income, aren't backed by any institution, and have no value to be depended upon. They are for the studied, specialized professional.

If you absolutely, positively must own gemstones as an investment, do yourself the favor of getting a vacation when you go out to buy them. There's a man of excellent reputation in the vacation spot of Cozumel, Mexico, who would be glad to sell you cut gems, on which you pay no import duties. His name is Martin C. P. Bernt, and he can be found in his emporium, Santa Cruz, on the northeast corner of the downtown square in Cozumel. If you can't visit in person, correspond at:

Santa Cruz
Avenida Juarez 117
P.O. Box 28
Cozumel, Mexico
(phone: 20982)

For additional reading, consult *The Dow Jones-Irwin Guide to Gems and Fine Jewelry* by David Marcum.[1]

ART AND COLLECTIBLES

Again, such esoterica are for professionals. Not long ago when inflation soared, people realized nice gains from art, vases, rugs, rare wines, stamps, coins, antiques, old cinema posters, comic books, and bubble gum cards. Most of us simply don't know enough to invest in these things, and amateurs have made money because they were soundly advised or because there was a greater fool who took them off their hands at a higher price. Buying them for their enjoyment value is one thing, but buying them for resale is another. Fortunately, most of these investments are extraordinarily expensive, and fortunately, also, most of us rebel against paying hundreds of dollars for a comic book.

If you must invest in such things, try lying down until the impulse passes. That failing, consult reputable dealers. Be advised, though, that dealers are more likely to appreciate the collector than the speculator. The rule for small investors is buy *objets d'art* because you want to live with them, not because they're investments.

FOREIGN CURRENCIES

During the 1970s people who had a Swiss franc or German mark left over from travels were astonished at how those cur-

---

[1] Homewood, Ill. Dow Jones-Irwin, 1986.

rencies had appreciated against the dollar. More recently, investors who opened high-interest savings accounts in Mexican banks were astounded at what a few devaluations could do to their wealth despite high Mexican interest rates. Betwixt the Swiss franc and the Mexican peso lies a world of woe for investors.

The money in foreign exchange is made by professional traders who monitor markets and reams of economic data and who have the backing to withstand setbacks. Private investors can participate in futures markets, buying long and selling short currencies, but this, too, requires substantial capital—to say nothing of iron nerves.

For the small investor, substantial profit may be outside economic reach. However, investment banking houses now offer certificates of deposit denominated in foreign currencies. These investments are advertised in the financial press with addresses and phone numbers to satisfy inquiries. Frequently, these CDs require $10,000 minimums, but some are available in $5,000 and perhaps $1,000 minimums.

Another foreign exchange strategy for the small investor is opening a foreign bank account denominated in another currency. One could, for example, open a savings account in Switzerland and specify the deposit to be held in francs, or British pounds, German marks, Canadian dollars, French francs, or another currency.

Also, there is a mutual fund that invests in Swiss francs:

Permanent Portfolio Fund
207 Jefferson Square
P.O. Box 5847
Austin, Texas 78763
(phone: 800-531-5142
In Texas: 512-453-7558)

PENNY STOCKS

In every market there are stocks that rise not a paltry percent or 3 percent but soar like the contrails of rockets, doubling, redoubling, compounding the balance sheets of their owners. In the 1970s, those stocks were *penny shares*, named because of their low cost (below $10 and often literally pennies per share). These stocks are often called *penny mining shares* because many are issued by mineral companies, but penny shares are also prevalent among companies far removed from mining. Reflecting their mining heritage, however, many of these stocks are listed on regional exchanges in the American West, although the OTC and American Exchange have shares selling for cents.

There's no question that many investors have profited from buying them. When you can buy stocks for a dime, an investment of $1,000 will take you a long way when prices move. Conversely, a couple hundred shares of a stock representing a total investment of $100 won't generate too much of a loss if the position moves adversely.

The problem, as with any equity investment, is picking the stock that will prosper. Penny stock enthusiasts advise simple procedures for doing so: pick penny shares alphabetically, or stab a fork into the stock pages, or pick something that has an appealing name. They say haphazard selections are likely to do as well as analysis, and maybe they're right. Another option is to subscribe to services that recommend penny stocks. One is:

> *The Penny Stock Journal*
> Attn: Subscription Fulfillment Dept. BA-3
> P.O. Box 2009
> Mahopac, New York 10541

Another service is:

> *The CHEAP Investor*
> Mathews and Associates—Dept. M–11
> 36 King Arthur Court—Suite 10
> Northlake, Illinois 60164
> Matthews is correct
> (phone: 800-228-6505)

Mathews and Associates monitors its "The Blue Cheap Index" of low-priced shares, many of which have done well. The thing might be worth subscribing to for the editors' humor even though investment periodicals are no longer deductible on your federal 1040.

FOREIGN STOCKS AND BONDS

International investing is in vogue during the late 1980s for two reasons: growth in world bond and equity markets and performance.

In 1970, the U.S. share of world equity markets (both stocks and bonds) measured in market value was 66 percent. By 1986, the figure was 45 percent. That happened because a greater number of countries opened capital markets (Korea and China, for instance), because existing markets grew (Paris and Tokyo and Singapore, especially), and because they proved to be lucrative sources of income.

American investors can purchase shares in foreign companies if they trade on U.S. exchanges. A good example is SONY Corp., listed on the NYSE. In this situation, investors actually purchase American depository receipts, or ADRs, which represent an equity investment in a foreign firm that's accessible through U.S. exchanges. ADRs are liquid like stocks.

In addition, private investors can purchase shares listed on foreign exchanges through a U.S. broker who uses his or her firm's international desk to execute transactions on, for example, the Paris *Bourse.* You might, for instance, want to buy shares in a Swiss pharmaceutical firm traded in Zurich, or a German industrial firm traded in Frankfurt, and you can do so.

The same is true with foreign bonds. You can purchase them when they're occasionally marketed in the United States, or you can instruct your broker to go buy them in Finland or South Africa or wherever.

But the best way for the small investor to diversify beyond U.S. shores is through a mutual fund specializing in foreign securities. International funds have proliferated madly in the past two years, and virtually every major mutual fund family has at least one foreign stock fund. Foreign bond funds have also sprouted up. Sometimes these international funds are a broad portfolio of stocks from all over the world, and sometimes they concentrate on specific geographical regions like the Pacific Basin. The performance of international funds has been exceptional. In 1986, for instance, international funds averaged a 43 percent total return compared with 16 percent for an average of all mutual funds.

REAL ESTATE

Is there a family in North or South America whose ancestors didn't have the chance to buy what's now downtown Miami? Not according to most families. Many people have garnered a bundle in real estate, but small investors would be wise to limit real estate holdings to the family residence. Those seeking greater participation in real estate have three other choices.

Purchase of rental property, like houses or condominiums, has remained relatively unscathed by tax reform. As of 1987 anyway, you still receive tax breaks from interest writeoffs and depreciation that can be charged against rental income. This is one of the few real estate investments that wasn't altered—if not destroyed—by tax reform, but remember that rental property entails much record-keeping, outlays for maintenance, and acceptance of illiquidity if you need to bail out during inopportune markets.

A real estate limited partnership used to be the most favored way to receive income and tax offsets from indirect investment in real estate. Under pre-1986 rules, you could use the partnership's tax offsets to charge against earned income. Unfortunately, tax aspects of real estate limited partnerships were struck severely by tax reform.

Many advisers say that real estate limited partnerships are now useful only for retired investors who select income-producing partnerships rather than tax-advantaged partnerships. Whether this advice is unchallengable is another question, but many partnership general managers are restructuring their offerings to concentrate on income properties rather than construction properties. Essentially, this means that real estate limited partnerships now compete with annuities, bonds, and other income investments formerly thought to be separate aspects of a portfolio. Minimum initial investment in limited partnerships is usually $5,000.

A real estate investment trust (REIT) is a company whose business is real estate. Investors buy stock in REITs as they would in any company. Many REITs are listed on public exchanges, but occasionally shares are offered in private placements available through a broker. As with any stock, REITs offer capital gains and dividends appropriate to their profitability, and profitability is linked to performance of real estate markets.

Real estate markets—and therefore REITs—are generally segmented into raw land, construction, and property management. Of the three, property management REITs are most suited for the lay investor, as they deal in existing, occupied buildings that have demonstrated cash flow.

Construction REITs were exceedingly popular during the late 1960s. Many of the most popular were bankrupt a few years later. Some of those that were bankrupted are back; some of their investors are, and some of them aren't.

CHAPTER FOURTEEN.

Working with Financial Advisers and Transaction Mechanics

Sorting among the thousands of potential advisers is a formidable task for the small investor, if for no other reason than everyone from your banker to your brother-in-law wants to tell you what to do with your money. Further, the development of national trading makes it possible for the small investor in Alabama to receive solicitation calls from Los Angeles or New York in addition to all the local advisers petitioning for attention. The small investor needs some means of culling among potential advisers, and the best place to begin is by realizing what certain categories of advisers can do for you.

INVESTMENT SPECIALISTS

First among broad categories of advisers is the investment specialist—a firm or individual who restricts activities to specific types of financial vehicles. An example of a corporation specializing in selected financial alternatives is Nuveen and Company, which specializes in municipal bonds. An example of individuals who work in a specialty might be a coin dealer, an insurance agent who handles annuities, or a broker in real estate or oil drilling partnerships.

Although versed in selected alternatives, these specialists do not serve a range of financial choices, and the small investor must be aware that these people deliberately restrict themselves to limited scopes. By choice, this category of potential adviser does not render general investment advice.

The specializing adviser can help you select among alternatives within his or her specialty, most likely can place orders for your account, and will probably provide continuing contact in monitoring your portfolio.

This isn't always the case, however. Some investment specialists merely act as agents for transactions and maintain records of your account, and they do not provide a sustained personal relationship. Their advisory capacity often is restricted to standard mailings that inform clients of market trends in their area of investment.

GENERALISTS

Specializing advisers can be useful to small investors, assuming you've decided to concentrate in the areas dealt in by specialists. Because the small investor needs diversification, however, you will probably be interested in advisers dealing in a range of investments. Investment generalists are of two types: personal financial planners and investment brokers.

Each type of investment generalist boasts certain credentials, ranging from the chartered financial analyst, who undergoes three years of testing and certification, to certified financial planners, who enroll in independent study courses for financial planning, to stockbrokers, called *registered representatives* because they must meet Securities and Exchange Commission registration requirements in order to act as agents for the public. Some of these generalists are highly educated and experienced, and others, of course, are novices with lesser skills and recommendation. The best way to determine a potential adviser's credentials is to ask for them.

Although many individuals have set themselves up in business as personal financial planners, these people usually deal with clients whose capital is far beyond the $5,000 we're working with. Therefore, small investors will find themselves dealing with representatives of institutions that provide general financial counsel, and even these people don't always take on clients of modest means. Unfortunately, small investors do not have the bankroll to attract high-powered advice, but financial houses are becoming receptive to small investors, and requirements for minimum account balances are falling.

One investment generalist who provides financial counsel to small investors is a bank or savings and loan officer. In the past, bankers didn't offer personal services except to their wealthiest depositors, but that's been changing as financial institutions intrude upon each other's former territory. Some banks even offer brokerage services, can direct you to real estate agents for purchase of property, and can act in capacities outside formerly restricted activities. Of course, banks still provide trust services, offer savings vehicles, and trade in government securities.

Lately large national financial institutions have been joining forces to provide broad investment services, and many of these services are accessible to small investors. Prudential-Bache, Shearson/American Express, and the Sears Financial Network are examples of combined forces prepared to discuss investment alternatives. These enterprises can be useful to the small investor. Typically, these financial networks execute transactions, maintain records, provide advice, and deal in a range of alternatives.

Selecting a personal financial adviser is still a matter of trial and error. You must locate an adviser who's willing to work with someone of limited capital and who is attuned to your stated needs. Even at this late date in financial history, many established advisers still work with prearranged formulas which they lay over anyone who walks in the door. As archaic as it sounds, word of mouth is probably the best way to locate an adviser, starting by asking friends in your economic situation whom they use as financial counsel and proceeding from there. Otherwise, the phone book will reveal sources of investment counsel in most locations.

STOCKBROKERS AND DISCOUNT BROKERS

Without doubt, the most useful—and most-used—of all investment advisers is the stockbroker. Unlike other investment advisers, stockbrokers must be affiliated with a brokerage house. In some cases, the brokerage will be a full-service organization, such as Dean Witter or PaineWebber, and in other cases the broker will be affiliated with a discount service, such as Rose and Company or Carl Schwab.

A broker affiliated with a full-service organization has at his or her disposal the resources of a sponsoring organization. Those resources include seats at the major stock exchanges and access to the OTC market and a legion of market analysts and supporting staff. Once you're a client of a full-service broker, expect continual calls advising you of selected investments, regular arrival of investment literature published by the broker's firm, and periodic evaluation of your holdings along with recommendations to add or delete securities. If your account and economic circumstances are substantial, a full-service broker will lend you money with which to buy securities.

The full-service brokerage also offers a broad array of investment vehicles, including mutual and money market funds, annuities, IRAs, CMAs, tax-deferred investments, and financial innovations as they're developed. In addition, full-service brokers may also trade commodities, deal in custodial accounts for minors, and undertake other transactions permitted by the Securities and Exchange Commission, the securities exchanges, and their firm.

In return for a full-service broker's time, resources, and attention, you pay substantial commissions. If the broker's recommendations are profitable, it will be worth the extra expense to have a formidable financial resources at your disposal. If not, you might be as well off with a discount broker.

We've mentioned discount brokers in several connections. A discount broker executes transactions and will place clients' names on market letter mailings. For the most part, however, discount brokers execute orders and maintain records and that's it. They offer no advice and few details other than price quotations. If you call a discount broker for advice, you'll be told bluntly that they don't provide it.

In exchange for reduced attention you pay lesser commissions. A discount broker typically charges a minimum commission of around $30 and, depending upon the size of your trade, ranging up to $200−$400. By contrast, a full-service broker's commissions start at about $100. A discount broker is not a financial adviser in the sense that we use the term. He or she provides access to securities markets. You make financial decisions without their counsel.

Although discount brokers usually provide the same access to markets as full-service brokers, there are some important omissions. Most, for example, do not trade in government securities and zero coupon CDs. Although a few discount brokers provide CMAs, most do not. Discount brokers offer self-directed IRAs, but many do not trade municipal bonds, annuities, and tax-advantaged investments, nor do they sponsor mutual funds or gold certificate programs. Thus, they are not a substitute for a full-service broker.

There's no limit to the number of brokerage accounts an individual may open, so many investors have accounts with full-service and discount brokers. From the former they receive advice and recommendations; from the latter, they receive execution of transactions.

DEALING WITH ADVISERS

Opening an account with a financial adviser, whether a financial services corporation or broker, is simple. In most cases, you must be employed full time, although that's not always required if you have ample part-time or unearned income. You must declare your salary, net worth exclusive of residence, and age. Some financial advisers require you to have a minimum salary and net worth, and some require investments of a specified minimum. Rarely, you may have to produce past years' federal income tax forms as confirmation of your income.

Opening an account is one thing, but dealing with your adviser or broker is a different matter. The most important point to remember is that in most cases an investment adviser is paid for making recommendations, not necessarily for making you money. The assumption is that you'll stop dealing with your adviser if recommendations aren't profitable, but remembering that your adviser is paid to sell services is an important step in evaluating recommendations.

In many cases, an adviser works for a firm which has an inventory of securities, and the adviser receives special favor from superiors for moving that inventory. If those securities happen to coincide with your needs, you and your adviser benefit. But once you buy an investment, your adviser has already made money. Whether you make money depends upon the wisdom of the investment.

It's important to remember that full-service brokers are fundamentally salespeople and secondarily investment counselors. Discount brokers, of course, are only order-takers and not advisers. All brokers make money by selling securities to you and for you. Whether those securities make you money or not, brokers get paid for the trade.

Given that your adviser is rarely paid on the basis of your gains, it's as important to know what you *don't* want to buy as it is to know what you do want to buy, because knowing what you don't want is an important aspect of sales resistance.

It's best to have a general category of investment in mind when dealing with an adviser so that you can provide initial guidelines. You might, for example, be interested in maximum current income, and you should indicate that during your initial conversation with a potential adviser. Your adviser will probably ask about your economic circumstances, and based upon your mutual assessment you might discover other needs. However, mutual discovery is more rewarding than saying, "I have $5,000. What do you suggest?"

After the two of you have settled upon general categories, you'll want to pick investments within those categories. In our example of the investor seeking maximum current income, stocks and bonds are likely to be the logical recommendations from an adviser—or in the case of readers dealing with discount brokers, you may already have determined stocks and bonds are the preferred choice for current income.

TRANSACTION TERMS

As the introduction said, advice on picking individual securities is beyond our immediate purpose, and that's one subject on which a financial adviser can be most useful. However, once you and your adviser—or you alone—have decided upon a particular investment, you need to know the language in which trades are executed. For the most part, those terms involve the price you'll pay for securities.

In the case of mutual funds, we saw that price was net asset value. The investor who, in conjunction with an adviser or by personal choice, selects a mutual fund investment will pay NAV per share plus loads or commissions if applicable. The fund's telephone representatives provide quotations of NAV. Investors can accept that price, or they can wait, hoping NAV will fall, permitting them to purchase more shares at the lower price.

Investors purchasing individual stocks or bonds have more latitude when it comes to specifying the price they pay for securities. In determining the current price of a publicly traded security, investors will call a broker and request a quotation for the security of interest. At this point, the conversation becomes a bit arcane.

The broker will dial up the security on a computer terminal and, in the case of a stock, reply something like "16 to an eighth, 16 last at 10,000." This code reveals the bid price, the asked price, the price of the most recent trade, and the sales volume. This oral information is the basis of the printed trading statistics we covered in chapters on stocks and bonds.

We became acquainted with bid and asked prices in the discussions of OTC stocks and government bonds. We noted that these quotes represent the price at which a securities dealer will buy (bid) and sell (ask) a security. Although traders in OTC securities and USGs are the most common sources of bid and asked prices, stocks traded on the New York or American exchanges are also handled by specialists who make markets in securities. The price you're quoted is the price at which these specialists are making markets.

In our example, we're told "16 to an eighth." That is, the bid price is $16 per share, and the asked price—that which you'd pay to buy a security—is $16⅛ ($16.125—remember?). The comment "16 last" indicates the most recent trade took place at $16 per share. "At 10,000" indicates that many shares have exchanged hands up to that point in the trading day—which, by the way, is 10 A.M. to 4 P.M. New York City time.

Bond quotations are delivered with similar brevity. You'll hear something like "80 to a quarter," meaning that the bid is $800 per bond and the asking price is $802.50, plus accrued interest in both cases.

After receiving this intelligence, you have several responses available. One, of course, is to say "thank you" and hang up the phone. Assuming, however, that you wish to purchase the security in question, you may either accept the ask price, or you may place an order for the security at a lesser price. Such was not the case, remember, with mutual funds.

PLACING ORDERS

If the quoted price is reasonable according to your or your adviser's assessment of worth, you may place a *market order* for the security. You simply say, "I'll take 100 (or however many) shares (or a specified number of bonds) at the market." This communication informs the broker that you're willing to buy a given number of shares or bonds at the prevailing market price. The broker will execute the transaction, and you will pay the market price at the moment of transaction.

However, prices change, and in placing a market order you acknowledge willingness to pay whatever price the market establishes. It may be, therefore, that your order will be executed at, say, $16.25 because the market price increased during your conversation with the broker. You did not specify the price of 16⅛; you said the market price would be fine with you, and if the market price increased, so be it.

If price uncertainties disturb you, you may issue a *limit order*. Limit orders specify the price at which you're willing to purchase a security, and your order will not be executed unless your security trades at that price "or better."

Say you place a limit order for 100 shares at $16 per share. You inform the broker, "I'll take 100 shares at 16 or better." The broker will process your order, but it will not be executed until your price of $16 is struck. The annotation "or better" is customary but unnecessary. All you're saying is it's OK to buy the stock at less than $16 per share if possible.

Market orders are executed immediately by the broker's representative on the trading floor of the exchange or upon conversation with the market maker in the case of orders placed Over the Counter. In some cases, your order can be placed while you wait, and before you hang up the phone your trade will be executed. In contrast, limit orders for prices must be accompanied by a time limit.

One type of limit order is the *fill or kill*, although more frequently this limit order is used in commodity trading. A fill or kill is a one-time shot. In issuing a fill or kill order, you are saying to a broker, "Place the order at this price, and if it isn't executed immediately, forget it."

A *day order* expires at the end of the trading day. If the specified price you wish to pay is not achieved by the end of the trading day, your limit order expires, and the trade isn't executed. By the same token, *week orders* and *month orders* are good for the periods implied. If your indicated price is reached during the trading week or month, the trade is executed. If the price isn't reached before the end of the week or month, the limit order expires.

One type of limit order that has no expiration is the *good 'til canceled* order, also called an *open order* or *GTC*. A GTC order informs your broker that your willingness to purchase a stock or bond at your specified price is in force until the order is executed or until you cancel it. Thus, the time period is indefinite, and in practice GTC orders have waited years before being executed.

Market and limit orders apply to sale as well as purchase of securities. You may place a market order to sell a stock or bond, which informs your broker that you want the securities sold immediately. As with all market orders, the emphasis is upon completing the transaction, not upon price. A limit order to sell informs the broker that you want to receive a specific price for the security. The same time considerations applying to limit orders to buy pertain to limit orders to sell.

A special type of limit order applying to sale of securities is the *stop loss order* or *stop order*. The purpose of *stops* is to protect sellers against declines in price by placing an order to sell a security if its price falls to a certain level. Say, for example, that you own 100 shares of AT&T selling at $25 per share. You can place a stop loss order to sell if the price falls to, say, $22, thereby preventing further losses.

Market and limit orders may be used with both stocks and bonds. However, in buying or selling stocks in units less than round lots of 100 shares—19 shares, 101 shares—odd-lot differentials apply, and that affects limit orders.

ODD LOTS

We've already covered the odd-lot differential. We noted that transactions of, say, 50 shares, cost one "bit" (⅛th of a point or 12.5 cents) per share more to buy and bring one bit less when selling. This means that limit orders to *buy* will be executed only when the stock is selling at ⅛th point *below* the purchase price. Limit orders to *sell* will be executed when the stock is selling at ⅛th point *above* your specified price.

Say you place a limit order to buy 50 shares of AT&T at $25 per share. Fifty shares is an odd lot, meaning you'll be charged 12.5 cents per share to purchase 50 shares. Therefore, your order to buy at $25 won't be executed until the price of AT&T strikes 24⅞, because the odd-lot differential will be charged. You still pay $25 per share, but you must be aware that the transaction won't take place until AT&T reaches $24.875 per share.

Conversely, if you place a limit order to sell at $25, your order will be filled when AT&T reaches 25⅛. You still receive the $25 per share, but the odd-lot differential applies, and the transaction won't be executed until the differential is accommodated by the price of the stock.

A good financial adviser will inform you of all costs and risks in an investment. If a potential adviser is reluctant or impatient in discussing costs, risks, commissions, and fees, perhaps he or she may handle your portfolio with similar reluctance or disinterest. Unfortunately, advisers can be judged only by performance, and that means judged according to how their recommendations work out. There are, however, ways you can appraise a potential adviser before doing business.

At the risk of belaboring, it is worthwhile to ask an adviser how he or she is compensated. The best compensation from the investor's viewpoint is for an adviser to receive a percentage of your gains from investment. This reduces your return, but your adviser doesn't make money if you don't, so it's in his or her interest for you to make money. In most cases, even if an adviser's main income is generated by gains from your account, maintenance fees and commissions are also charged, meaning your adviser will be paid for handling your portfolio even if it doesn't make money for you. And in many cases it is not legal for an adviser to be paid a percentage of your gains.

Next, inquire about performance of a potential adviser's past recommendations. This is like asking a potential employee for references—you're not going to hear anything unfavorable—but you might receive some clue as to past successes. You'll be especially interested in knowing his or her experience in handling clients of your financial size.

Another trick is to follow an adviser's recommendations without actually putting your money on the table. Simply follow price movements of the recommended investment in *The Wall Street Journal*. This may cost you profits you could have been earning, but it will give you another indication of an adviser's savvy, and if the recommendation is making money, you'll have confidence in future advice.

After you've chosen an adviser and started trading, you'll evaluate advice you're receiving by the profits you're making. However, there are a couple other measures you can employ.

First, keep track of how long your adviser will let a position turn against you before he or she recommends you dump an investment and put money elsewhere. Conscientious advisers monitor your downside and establish a level beyond which they'll suggest you get out.

Second, keep track of how often your adviser urges you to alter composition of your portfolio. The long-term investor shouldn't be moving money around every few months, but frequent trades mean more commissions and more returns to your adviser. Frequent buy and sell recommendations are called *account churning,* and their purpose is to generate commissions.

Third, monitor how faithfully your adviser adheres to your investment goals. If he or she calls frequently with recommendations that don't meet objectives you discussed, you're being treated as another customer, not an individual.

Fourth, remember how often your adviser apprises you of new investments that *do* meet your objectives.

Fifth, note how mechanics of your account are serviced. Matters such as how efficiently trades are executed and how promptly dividends and interest are credited to your account are becoming highly important as volume of securities trading swells and brokerage back rooms are pressed to process everything accurately. Your adviser will provide regular account statements, but it's your responsibility to assure accuracy. You must monitor the progress of your investments, keeping track of dividend and interest dates, purchases and sales, and other particulars to make sure all is recorded accurately in your account.

CERTIFICATES AND PROXIES

One important aspect of account mechanics is custody of securities certificates, documents certifying your ownership of an investment. More frequently in recent years, evidence of ownership is recorded on computer tape, and your personal documentation will be recorded on your account statements. T-bills, mutual funds, and unit trusts, as well as some municipal bonds, zeros, and annuities, are kept track of in this fashion, with computers watching other computers to see you get what's yours.

However, certificates evidencing ownership of stocks and bonds are issued, and you must decide whether you want them in custody of your adviser or to take possession of them. Both possibilities have merit.

A broker or adviser can keep your certificates, holding them in *street name*. Under this arrangement, your broker or adviser knows you're the owner of record, but his or her firm is listed as the owner in the issuer's records. It's up to your adviser to see that returns are properly credited to your account and that you are informed of matters pertaining to your status as owner.

The advantage in holding securities in street name is the convenience of buying and selling without having physically to deal with paper certificates, as explained in a moment. Disadvantages may outweigh this advantage.

First, the corporation in which you bought stock doesn't know you're the owner. It can't contact you directly if it needs to, as it might in informing you of matters pertaining to your ownership. One such matter is the voting of your shares. You'll remember that stock ownership makes you an owner of a corporation and entitles you to a voice in some affairs of the corporation. Your voice is exercised through voting a proxy.

Whenever matters requiring shareholder approval are brought before directors, the corporation is obliged to solicit your vote. Such matters as selection of independent auditors, approval of stock splits, stock compensation plans for management, confirmation of the board of directors, and adoption of certain public policies require shareholder vote.

That vote is solicited by mailing you a proxy statement outlining issues to be decided. You complete the proxy card with your vote and mail it back in a preaddressed envelope. Your vote is tallied by an independent agent and recorded for or against each measure in question. If the corporation can't reach you directly because your stock is held in street name, your vote may be delayed. In short, your adviser's holding your securities may short-circuit your role in corporate democracy.

Second, if your adviser or broker is listed as owner of the security, dividends and interest payments are mailed to him or her. That will be fine if you instruct your broker to reinvest proceeds immediately in one of his or her firm's money funds.

If you hold stock and bond certificates personally, you are listed as the owner in the corporation's records, and all dividends, interest, and proxy materials are mailed to you at the address of record. Investors typically register securities as individuals or joint tenants. The former status means one person holds sole claim to dividends, interest, and capital appreciation from the security. The latter status indicates shared ownership, and it's commonly used by married couples who hold assets together, although nothing prevents you and a friend or another relative from owning securities as joint tenants.

Other forms of registration are allowed. For instance, investors who purchase securities for IRAs must have them registered to an intermediary. Parents may establish trusts with a bank, in which case the bank maintains control of certificates, dividends, and interest. Also, accounts for minors are registered to the minor's custodian.

Registration is established at the time you open an account with an adviser or broker. If you open a single account, your securities will be registered in individual ownership. If you open a joint account, joint ownership will be indicated on your stock or bond certificate. You may have as many accounts as you wish, with a single broker or adviser or with many.

In these days when couples are marrying later, divorcing frequently, and pursuing separate investment goals for reasons of temperament, design, or attention to taxes, it's common for brokers to carry his, her, and their accounts. Just make sure you specify which account you're trading when you place the buy or sell order.

When you sell securities held personally, you must fill out the back of the stock or bond certificate and return it to your adviser or broker. Usually brokerages will include instructions for completing the back of the certificate along with confirmation of the sell order. You must fill in your social security number, complete the blank authorizing a particular agent to execute the sale, and date and sign the certificate precisely as registered on the front. Both parties must sign in the case of joint ownership.

So long as you hold the certificate, you may sell through any agent of your choice. You can buy securities through one adviser and sell through another, and many investors do so. They may, for example, buy securities through a full-service broker, paying higher commissions warranted by the broker's advice, and sell through a discount broker, paying lower commissions, because they've decided to sell without counsel and don't feel obligated to pay full-service brokers for advice not rendered.

KEEPING INFORMED

For the investor who doesn't require personal contact with an adviser, there are investment advisory services which correspond with clients through the mails and on occasion offer a "hot line" to apprise clients of moves in monitored investments. These advisories run the range of alternatives. Some deal in precious metals, others in stocks, still others in "market timing," movement of money from one investment to another.

Often these mail advisories provide specific recommendations on purchase and sale of selected investments, as was the case with advisories dealing in penny stocks mentioned in the previous chapter. Most will offer an opinion about the investment climate in general along with recommendations. Cost ranges from a few dollars per year to a thousand dollars or more, with the Value Line Investment Survey, which provides exhaustive analysis of stocks, ranking toward the top in prestige and cost. Fortunately, Value Line is available through libraries and business colleges.

An advisory of similar distinction and lesser cost is offered by Standard & Poor's Corporation. S&P is a far-reaching investment organization that rates bonds and preferred stocks, runs indexes of market performance, and provides evaluations of stocks for professional and personal investors.

The S&P 500 Stock Market Encyclopedia and *The S&P Outlook* are useful for small investors. The former is an extended reference work detailing financial particulars and market past of 500 stocks comprising the S&P 500 Index. The latter is a continuing update on market activity and forecast which "offers informed recommendations on how you can preserve or enhance the value of your personal portfolio."

Periodically, Standard & Poor's offers introductory subscriptions to its services. By subscribing to the *Outlook* for three months at the trial subscription price of $29.95, you also receive the *Encyclopedia* and a list of recommended stocks. You can try out both publications by sending $29.95 to

> The Outlook
> Standard & Poor's Corporation
> Box 992
> New York, NY 10275

One advisory service of merit to mutual fund investors is Prime Investment Alert. Prime advises investors on moving holdings among mutual fund families by using switch privileges. It also offers the Prime Tax Alert service, which, by its advertisement, "will provide timely tax advice and creative ways to save on taxes." The cost for both services is $100 per year for monthly mailings, occasional special reports, and a telephone hot line, but Prime offers a first-year subscriber rate of $60. The address is:

Prime Investment Alert
P.O. Box 10300
Portland, Maine 04104
(phone: 207-772-1679)

There's still worthwhile free advice to be had, and one of the most informative and amusing sources is the public television program "Wall $treet Week" featuring Louis Rukeyser and panelists who are major money managers. Mr. Rukeyser and guests offer commentary and stock selections each Friday evening, although their discussions rarely include other investments. Further, most major corporations subscribe to financial services such as Merrill Lynch or Chase Econometrics, and maybe you can have yourself placed on the inter-office mailing list. This additional reading may be as useful as personal counsel.

Finally, there's one organization that devotes itself to the small investor exclusively. It is the American Association of Individual Investors, a nonprofit educational corporation that publishes a monthly magazine discussing investments, provides investment seminars at modest cost to members, and generally caters to small investors. A one-year membership is $48. The address is:

American Association of Individual Investors
612 North Michigan Avenue
Chicago, IL 60611
(phone: 312-280-0170)

SUMMARY

In conclusion, the small investor doesn't have to enter the investment maze without a guide. Professionals and professional publications of diverse sorts are willing to offer guidance, and they're easy to work with so long as you know what they're about and the language they speak. Even though small investors must bear the costs and risks of investing, there are legions of advisers to offer recommendations, and given luck and intelligence from all parties, all of you can make money.

The Apollonian Investor

This is the part of the book your author likes best—the conclusion, which isn't a closing but an enlargement upon everything that's come before.

In the preceding pages we've raised lots of alternatives available to the investor of modest capital. Unfortunately, we've not discussed the most important aspect of investing, the aspect which, ignored, makes all choices unproductive. Investing is more than selecting rationally among alternatives available for $5 to $5,000. Regrettably, investing is also a statement of personality, an expression of one's attitude about money and its importance in life, a commentary we make about ourselves. Your author writes "regrettably" because most people don't consider who they are before putting their money somewhere.

It may seem a strange point to raise, but the latter-day "Adam Smith" wrote great wisdom in this sentence from *The Money Game:* "If you don't know who you are, this is an expensive place to find out."

"Ridiculous," you say.

Maybe, and maybe not.

Our book has been devoted to the meat and potatoes investor, the man or woman who, regardless of education or age, has a bit of money to invest and wants to earn returns on it. That, you may have discovered in life, isn't everyone.

The father of a close friend *invests* on every hot tip he hears, never considering that he lives a far throw from any financial center, isn't associated with professional investments, and nearly always ends up riding the dying *investment* into the ground while those starting the rumor have long since sold out and moved on. "I thought I had inside information," he says, surveying his losses.

Clearly, this man wants something else from his investments. Perhaps he wants the illusion of being an insider, or perhaps he'd rather have one large gain instead of many steady gains, or perhaps a psychological script motivates his investments. The point is that he's serving other agenda in his investments, and they aren't in line with his reality.

In contrast, there's a professor of finance at a Big Ten university whose salary is a pittance of her investment income. She's well respected in her field, which is commodities and option trading, and she's well liked by her colleagues because, after running the analyses of her recondite profession, she often turns profitable recommendations over to colleagues with the explanation, "This just isn't my kind of stock." She's foregone income, but that woman has nothing she's trying to prove through a portfolio.

In short, we all have an attitude about investments whether we realize it openly or not, and we all have fantasies—there's nothing deluding about fantasies; they're dreams of what could be—about ourselves and money. In your quiet moments, you'll admit them to yourself.

Some of us indulge the fantasy of clawing our way atop the investment ladder and then retiring to contemplation like Lao Tsu, a wealthy Chinese merchant who wrote *The Book of Tao* before disappearing into Tibet aback a water buffalo thousands of years ago.

The rest of us consider less extreme alternatives which allow us to remain in the material world to enjoy what we've accumulated. That preference places us in a different tradition—closer to that of the Golden Age Greeks, actually.

These days, Jimmy the Greek and Zorba the Greek and Aristotle Onassis are about all who are cited from the Agean greatness, but once upon a time immortals strode the earth there. One was Apollo, god of grace and harmony, who lent his name—Apollonian—to all that was measured and mellifluous, poetic, and peaceful. Another was Dionysus, god of wine and

wenching, a zesty fellow whose name—Dionysian—is synony-
mous with revelry and intoxication.

Economists and market observers have forgotten about
Apollo and Dionysus. You're not likely to pick up the paper and
read:

"Federal Reserve Board Chairman Paul Volker assured
Congress today that Ml-A would continue its Apollonian pace
throughout the remainder of the third fiscal quarter."

Or:

"The Dow Jones Industrial Average sprinted 23 points at
today's opening bell before retreating to a new yearly low,
continuing its Dionysian fluctuations for the third consecutive
week."

That doesn't mean, however, that Apollo and Dionysus
aren't still up there somewhere, grinning down upon human
folly. And, if you look closely, they still intrude themselves
between the lines of investment literature.

Early in 1983, James D. Robinson, III, chairman of American
Express Company, was featured in a full-page advertisement in
The Wall Street Journal. He was exhorting other CEOs to start
corporate savings bond drives. "I think these Savings Bonds
should be in every portfolio, including yours," he told his
fellow chairmen, adding, "The least your employees can do is
double their money in 10 years."

About the same time, one of the nation's largest brokerages
was soliciting customers with a brochure that announced in
stunning red ink: "Remember—$500 doubled every year is
$1,000,000 in ten years."

Mathematically, both are in the same ballpark (the brokerage was a bit off; it takes slightly longer), but mythologically
they're on different teams. Mr. Robinson was advocating Apollonian investing—the steady return, no churning of portfolios,
the graceful, predictable long-term doubling of money with no
intoxicating riding of markets—whereas the brokerage was
Dionysian—doubling your money every year for a decade is
going to take investors for wild rides if not disasterous spills.

The question is: Which are you—really?

Dionysian investors are likely to follow the adage offered by
an investment counselor in the heady 1960s stock market: "Put
all your eggs in one basket, and watch the basket like a hawk."

Apollonian investors prefer the original quotation: "Don't put all your eggs in one basket."

Spreading your financial eggs among holdings is called *portfolio management*, and, in case you haven't figured it out by now, Apollo has been reading over your shoulder as we've reviewed the possibilities available to small investors. True to our opening chapters, we've been looking at stable and predictable returns from investments, and the time has come now to look at combining some of the possibilities we've laid out— forming an Apollonian portfolio, as it were.

The purpose of a portfolio as opposed to a single investment is to diversify holdings in order to achieve several purposes. In general, those purposes are capital preservation, current income, and capital growth.

Those purposes serve different needs, and the kind of portfolio you construct depends upon your needs, which depend upon many factors—age, number of dependents, job security and profitability, spending habits, tax bracket, additional sources of income, and personal temperament. No single portfolio will serve all people, and even persons in similar circumstances prefer different portfolios. Instead of constructing portfolios for each type of investor, it's easier to consider which investments we've examined meet which purpose. You can then tilt your portfolio to accommodate your needs. So let's review the following considerations.

STABILITY OF PRINCIPAL

The purpose of this category of investments is to avoid market loss, and constant-dollar investments meet this need.

The most obvious among such investment vehicles are conventional savings accounts, time deposits, and certificates of deposit. You'll remember that these vehicles provide governmentally backed guarantees and guaranteed rates of interest. They also provide current income or reinvestment of interest for compounding.

An investment of greater return and equal stability is the money market fund from a depository institution, a broker, or a mutual fund. These constant-dollar funds provide competitive rates of interest as well as liquidity. Money funds concentrating in corporate investments provide good returns. Investors seeking maximum security can choose money funds specializing in government securities, and investors for whom high taxes are important can select a constant-dollar municipal fund.

Other choices for stability of principal are government, municipal, and corporate bonds maturing within a year or two. Because of their short maturities, these instruments won't fluctuate greatly in price. Also, savings bonds don't fluctuate in price.

MAXIMUM CURRENT INCOME

Investors desiring maximum current income generally prefer to invest in stocks and bonds.

Bonds have offered handsome interest payments for many years, and with the range of maturities available they can do so for many years to come. Many common and preferred stocks, especially those of public utilities, offer attractive dividends. Many mutual funds specialize in high-yield stocks and bonds for those seeking current income, and investors may choose to receive mutual fund distributions in cash rather than reinvesting in additional shares.

LONG-TERM GROWTH IN CAPITAL

The long-term investor has many options also. Zero coupon bonds as well as conventional corporate and government bonds selling at discounts from par offer the opportunity for predictable growth in capital. The EE savings bond can be useful for long-term appreciation, as can annuities, guaranteed return plans, and mutual funds with long-term growth as their objective.

Individual ownership of corporate stocks can also provide steady growth, if you're a wise picker among issues. Also, many precious metal investors contend that gold and silver offer superb prospects for long-term growth. Corporate pension and profit sharing plans also fit into this category.

AGGRESSIVE CAPITAL APPRECIATION

Investors after sharp gains can do well during stock market euphoria, either as direct owners of securities or as holders of shares in mutual funds pursuing a fast buck. The small investor is probably better off pursuing this Dionysian goal through a fund.

LUMP-SUM ACCUMULATIONS

The lump-sum component of the portfolio is devoted to accumulating predictable quantities of funds within a known period. Retirement planning, paying for a child's college education, launching a business, planning to cover a ballon payment on a mortgage—all of these financial events are part of the lump-sum component of the portfolio.

Zero coupon investments are ideally suited for the lump-sum component, and here again your author can be of service in helping you deal with this aspect of your investment program. Your author's third book *The Dow Jones-Irwin Guide to Zero Coupon Investments*,[1] is a comprehensive guide to all types of zero coupon investments and their use in a total portfolio.

Let's look for a moment at how different investors might construct Apollonian portfolios.

The beginning investor who can muster only a few hundred dollars lacks the versatility to accommodate all four investment objectives. Therefore, he or she will probably decide to open a conventional savings account or a no-minimum money market fund. Doing so will permit accumulation of a critical mass of investment capital eventually.

Other options include EE savings bonds and stock mutual funds requiring low-minimum investments, perhaps only $250 to $500. Also it's not out of the question that the beginning investor might wish to purchase precious metal coins or bullion and stop off at a bank to buy a little foreign currency. Also, some corporate stock plans permit employees to become involved for as little as $25 per month.

---

[1]Homewood, Ill.: Dow Jones-Irwin, 1986.

Investors with, say $1,000, can continue the minimal portfolio, enlarging selected elements as needs demand and conditions permit, or they might prefer to accumulate a larger capital mass via the somewhat higher interest afforded by time certificates.

One particular mutual fund of use to the $1,000 investor is the Permanent Portfolio Fund mentioned in the previous chapter. The fund maintains fixed portions of its holdings in gold, silver, Swiss francs, real estate and natural resource stocks, T-bills, and selected American securities. It permits diversification across investment vehicles as well as the standard advantages of mutual funds.

Investors with several thousand dollars can apportion assets into many areas. They may continue relying upon mutual funds and money funds for growth and stability, or they may decide to branch into direct ownership of securities. Whatever their decision, they can afford to disperse their holdings among stocks, bonds, and other vehicles if they choose. Their choice in doing so will depend upon the personal considerations discussed earlier.

For example, investors in or near retirement will want maximum current income from their portfolios, bearing in mind that they can't risk heavy losses but also need some growth because life expectancies have increased. These investors will likely alter portfolios away from aggressive capital gains investments toward high-income stocks, bonds, and mutual funds, relying upon deep discount bonds and equity funds for capital gains plus income.

Similarly, other investors with high demands upon current income—those with children, for example—may prefer some combination of income and growth, while their children may need portfolios that provide accumulations of steady growth to be expended in tuition or another lump-sum single purpose. The parents are likely to find themselves in growth and income mutual funds, whereas the kids are likely to be accumulating CATS and TIGRs along with other pets.

They're in a different situation from midcareer professionals who may seek maximum capital growth because they can afford a few financial bumps along the way. On the other hand, such fast-track professionals may find themselves better off by accumulating as many of their company's shares as possible, meaning they're heavily invested in their corporate stock plans.

All of these considerations are important in managing your personal portfolio, and you'll find them discussed in your author's second book *Life Cycle Investing*.[2] It's the second step in your investment education.

We've come quite a spell since our introduction. Along the way we've diverted ourselves with financial forays into obscure places before ending up on Mount Olympus. Some may find the journey strange, but Mr. Graham, the classics student, author of *The Intelligent Investor*, would approve. They say that everybody has to be somewhere, and now all of us have to be elsewhere. Until we meet again—perhaps between the covers of your author's two additional personal investment books— may you have the best of luck with your investments.

---

[2]Homewood, Ill.: Dow Jones-Irwin, 1986.